Insuring Healthcare Dynamics

Abdullah Samad

CONTENTS

CHAPTER – I

INTRODUCTION

1.1 INTRODUCTION

From the ancient times, human beings have been interested in trying to cure disease. The magician, priests, medicine man and the herbalist have all formulated various ways to cure man's disease and/or to bring relief to the sick. Though there was an almost complete absence of scientific medical knowledge, it would not be fair to say that the early practitioners of medicine contributed nothing to the alleviation of man's suffering from disease.

Medical knowledge in fact has been derived, to a very great degree, from the experimental and observational propositions and cumulative experiences gleaned from others. A history of medicine thus contributes a review of accomplishments and errors, false theories and misinformation and mistaken interpretations. It is also a study of the evolution of man and of human knowledge down the ages; of the biographies of eminent individuals who developed medicine; of the discoveries and inventions in different historical periods; and of the ever-changing concepts, goals and objectives of medicine. In the course of its evolution, which proceeded by stages, with advances and halts, medicine has drawn richly from the traditional cultures of which it is a part, and later from biological and natural sciences and more recently from social and behavioral sciences. Medicine is thus built on the best of the past. In the crucible of time, medicine has evolved itself into a social system heavily bureaucratized and politicized. The "explosion" of knowledge' during the 20th century has made

1

medicine more complex, and treatment more expensive, but the benefits of modern medicine have not yet penetrated the social periphery in many countries. The glaring contrasts in the state of health between the developed and developing countries, between the rural and urban areas, and between the rich and poor have attracted worldwide criticism as "social injustice". The commitment of all countries, under the aegis of World Health Organization, is to wipe out the inequalities in the distribution of health resources and services, and attain the Millennium Development Goals. The goal of modern medicine is no longer merely treatment of sickness. The other and more important goals which have emerged are prevention of disease, promotion of health and improvement of the quality of life of individuals and groups or communities. In other words, the scope of medicine has considerably broadened during recent years. It is also regarded as an essential component of socio-economic development.

1.2 PUBLIC HEALTH

The public health concept was born in England around 1840. Earlier, Johanna Peter Frank (1745-1821) a health philosopher of his time, conceived public health as good health laws enforced by the police and enunciated the principle that the State is responsible for the health of its people. The Public Health Act of 1848 was a fulfillment of his dream about the State's responsibility for the health of its people.

Cholera which is often called the "father of public health" appeared time and again in the western world during the 19th century. An English epidemiologist, John Snow, studied the epidemiology of cholera in London from 1848 to 1854 and established the role of polluted drinking water in the spread of cholera. In 1856, William Budd, another pioneer, by careful observations of an outbreak of typhoid

2

fever in the rural north of England concluded that the spread was by drinking water, not by miasma arid sewer gas. These two discoveries were all the more remarkable when one considers that the causative agents of cholera and typhoid fever were not identified. Then came the demand from people for clean water. At that time the Thames was both a source of drinking water and the depository for sewage. A comprehensive piece of legislation was brought into force in England, the Public Health Act of 1875 for the control of man's physical environment. The torch was already lit by Chadwick, but the man who was actually responsible more than any other for sanitary reforms was Sir John Simon (1816-1904), the first medical officer of health of London. He built up a system of public health in England which became the admiration of the rest of the world.[1] This early phase of public health (1880-1920) is often called the "disease control phase". Efforts were directed entirely towards general cleanliness, garbage and refuse disposal. Quarantine conventions were held to contain disease.

The development of the public health movement in America follows closely the English pattern. In 1850, Lemuel Shattuck (1793-1859), a bookseller and publisher, published his report on the health conditions in Massachusetts. Like. Chadwick's report it stirred the conscience of the American people to the improvement of public health. France, Spain, Australia, Germany, Italy, Belgium and the Scandinavian countries all developed their public health. By the beginning of the 20th century, the broad foundations of public health clean water, clean surroundings, wholesome condition of houses, control of offensive trades, etc were laid in all the countries of the western world. After the First World War, there were three particular newcomers to the public health scene Yugoslavia, Turkey and Russia.[2] These three countries in 1920 presented the typical picture of the underdeveloped world. Today they are quite advanced in public health.

While public health made rapid strides in the western world, its progress has been slow in the developing countries such as India where the main health problems continue to be those faced by the western world 100 years ago. The establishment of the WHO providing a Health Charter for all people provided a great fillip to the public health movement in these countries (1819-1901) who first mooted the concept of multifactorial causation of disease but his ideas were lost in the bacteriological era. The concept of multifactorial causation was revived by epidemiologists who have contributed significantly to our present-day understanding of multifactorial causation of disease and "risk-factors" in the etiology of disease.

1.3 CONCEPT OF HEALTH

Health is a common theme in most cultures. In fact, all communities have their concepts of health, as part of their culture. Among definitions still used, probably the oldest is that health is the "absence of disease". In some cultures, health and harmony are considered equivalent, harmony being defined as "being at peace with the self, the community, god and cosmos". The ancient Indians and Greeks shared this concept and attributed disease to disturbances in bodily equilibrium of what they called "humors".

Modern medicine is often accused for its preoccupation with the study of disease, and neglect of the study of health. Consequently, our ignorance about

4

health continues to be profound, as for example, the determinants of health are not yet clear; the current definitions of health are elusive; and there is no single yardstick for measuring health. There is thus a great scope for the study of the "epidemiology" of health.

Health continues to be a neglected entity despite lip service. At the individual level, it cannot be said that health occupies an important place; it is usually subjugated to other needs defined as more important, e.g., wealth, power, prestige, knowledge, security. Health is often taken for granted, and its value is not fully understood until it is lost. At the international level, health was "forgotten" when the covenant of the League of Nations was drafted after the First World War. Only at the last moment, was world health brought in. Health was again "forgotten" when the charter of the United Nations was drafted at the end of the Second World War. The matter of health had to be introduced ad hoc at the United Nations Conference at San Francisco in 1945.[3]

However, during the past few decades, there has been a reawakening that health is a fundamental human right and a worldwide social goal; that it is essential to the satisfaction of basic human needs and to an improved quality of life; and, that it is to be attained by all people. In 1977, the 30th World Health Assembly decided that the main social target of governments and WHO in the coming decades should be "the attainment by all citizens of the world by the year 2000 of a level of health that will permit them to lead a socially and economically productive life", for brevity, called "Health for All".[4] With the adoption of health as an integral part of socio-economic development by the United Nations in 1979,[5] health, while being an end in itself, has also become a major instrument of overall socio-economic development and the creation of a new social order.

1.4 DEFINITIONS OF HEALTH

"Health" is one of those terms which most people find it difficult to define although they are confident of its meaning. Therefore, many definitions of health have been offered from time to time, including the following:

a. "the condition of being sound in body, mind or spirit, especially freedom from physical disease or pain" (Webster);

b. "soundness of body or mind; that condition in which its functions are duly and efficiently discharged" (Oxford English Dictionary);

c. "a condition or quality of the human organism expressing the adequate functioning of the organism in given conditions, genetic and environmental";[6]

d. "a modus vivendi enabling imperfect men to achieve a rewarding and not too painful existence while they cope with an imperfect world";[7]

e. "a state of relative equilibrium of body form and function which results from its successful dynamic adjustment to' forces tending to disturb it. It is not passive interplay between body substance and forces impinging upon it but an active response of body forces working toward readjustment" (Perkins).

Health Economics is a branch of economics concerned with issues related to efficiency, effectiveness, value and behavior in the production and consumption of health and health care.

Health economics seeks to identify problem areas in a health care system and propose solutions for pressing issues by evaluating all possible causes and solutions.

1.5 HEALTH INSURANCE

Health insurance is an insurance against the risk of incurring medical expenses among individuals. By estimating the overall risk of health care expenses among a targeted group, an insurer can develop a routine finance structure, such as a monthly premium or payroll tax, to ensure that money is available to pay for the health care benefits specified in the insurance agreement. The benefit is administered by a central organization such as a government agency, private business, or not-for-profit entity.

Health insurance in a narrow sense would be 'an individual or group purchasing health care coverage in advance by paying a fee called *premium*.' In its broader sense, it would be any arrangement that helps to defer, delay, reduce or altogether avoid payment for health care incurred by individuals and households. Given the appropriateness of this definition in the Indian context, this is the definition, we would adopt.

Most developed countries have some kind of collective financing for health services, either through tax (e.g., the Health Service of the United Kingdom) or through their contributions to "social" health and the demand for Social Health Insurance. This type of insurance is usually characterized by mandatory membership, at least for the vast majority of the population, open enrollment, and community rating, i.e., a prohibition to charge premiums related to individual risk.

From a normative point of view, the institution of Social Health Insurance (SHI) can be defended on both Efficiency and equity grounds, whereas positive economics seeks to explain its existence in democracies on the basis of public choice models.

Historically the first political step toward Health insurance happened in Germany, in 1883 and followed in other European countries in twentieth century. The payment method in Germany was per capital and monthly some amount paid to physician according to the insured patient list.

From 1930 the conception of social insurance gradually was widespread and each country established its social insurance system based on traditional values, financial condition and ideological primaries.

The history of social insurance in developing countries is sketchy and not well known. The information about Asia, Middle East and North Africa is not clear but good information is available for Latin America.

In the third millennium the first concern for future of health insurance institutes is costs, while other elements including supplying services have second importance in institution charts. Increasing pressure on existing financial resources, it is inevitable to achieve strategic economical analyzes from different points. The governments are responsible to supply the most amount of financial resources in health care section.[8]

In supplying financial resources there are three absolute problems:

A. The costs of health care boosting constantly

B. Science and technology are boosting nonstop

C. World population trends indicate boosting

One of the criteria of developments in different countries is the scale of population fruition from social insurance.[9]

The health insurance market in India is very limited covering about 10% of the total population. The existing schemes can be categorized as:

(1) Voluntary health insurance schemes or private-for-profit schemes

(2) Employer-based schemes

(3) Insurance offered by NGOs/community based health insurance, and

(4) Mandatory health insurance schemes or government run schemes (namely ESIS, CGHS)

1.6 HEALTH ECONOMICS

Health economics has been defined by various authors in different terms. Analysis of some of the definitions suggest that health economics is the discipline that determines the quantity and price of scarce resources devoted for the care of the sick and promotion of health. It encompasses the medical 'industry as a whole and extends to such fields as the economic analysis of the cost of diseases, benefit of health programmes, returns from investments in medical education, training and research.

The definition laid down by the WHO inter-regional seminar seems to be more comprehensive. It defined health economics as that which seeks inter alia to quantify over times, the resources used in health service delivery, their organization functioning and the efficiency with which the resources allocated and used for health purposes and the effect of preventive curative and rehabilitative health services on individual and national productivity.

The health economy is essentially an application branch in economics which briefly can be divided into four sub branches; supplying financial recourses and insurance, hospital economy, labor force and general financial supply.

In developed countries health care cost covers 6 to 13 per cent of GNP while in developing countries it is less than 5 per cent. The World Health Organization ascertains the limit to 5 percent. Although "Health for all" is acceptable for all countries as a strategy but the necessary financial resources has not been foresighted.

For supplying financial recourses there are several solutions such as "Compulsory Insurance", "Supplying financial resources by tax revenue" and "Benefiting financial resources from non-government systems".[10]

Anne Mills the professor of London Health and Medical Colleague for tropical areas express a summery of progress in health economy for medium countries in three stages (decades 1970, 1980, and 1990) as following.

A. The health economical views before decades of 1970

Attention to economical activates in healthcare and welfare was started from the historical article by Gerry Rosenthal regarding Health & Society with emphasizing on historical trend in United States of America.

The root of economical health can be found in eighteen century in writing of Sir William Petty who was an economist and statistic expert and founder of political economy. Petty evaluated the worth of each person based on the services he or she offers to society. He says "It is not in benefit of government to leave sick and physician to themselves and avoid any help" (Petty, 1676).

In nineteenth century E. Chadwick could influence the law making about heath. He expressed, "Such as an artist who imagines a human being as beautified personalized statues and philologists according to his profession imagine human being merely as living statue, the economist also for boosting and development of his science can imagine human as a capitalist in productive forces.

He demonstrated that "building a bath is a good investment and prevention of diseases could be more useful than building a hospital".

In autumn of 1908 an infectious disease were prevailed in Punjab of India, the effects firstly appeared between railroad staffs by outbreak of fever and influenced the services! In all cities nearly all population were paralyzed, normal business deranged in all cities nearly , and the workers were sick for several weeks and even sellers were hindered from daily work.

B. The view about Health economy in decades of 1970

In this decade the difficulties and shortcomings of government for allocating of financial resources and using them efficiently sparked the technique of cost-revenue which helped the economists to discuss in this field. This technique in decades of 1950 to 1960 in decision about investments in health care then in investigation of disease influences on production was used. In 1970 also the same as previous decades the influences of health improvement on growing of

11

economy was emphasized with this difference that more emphasize was on investments in health care. The progress in techniques of economical evaluation for health section resulted in appearance of cost –effectiveness .This technique predominantly were used in measurable area.

Brian Able Smith says "Now the Cost –Effectiveness analysis is the main tool of improvement in health car system".

In latest years of 1970 a lot of research about evaluation were carried out which we here indicate two of them that reveal the usefulness of research about Cost –Effectiveness in politicizing and management of special fields.

Good Ferry, Walker and Oscar Gish investigated about the affects of using air plane in health car aid for far reaching areas of Botswana.

At that time using air planes were privileged in some African countries .Walker using some infectious information which were collected from remedied ills by physicians and other health care staffs.

C. The Health Economy Views in 1980

1980 can be named the period of supplying financial resources for health car .In this decade the economists after confirmation of economical conception relations in health car systems tried to estimate the demand functions and using them for determining the cost disease policies.

The private sector was in center of observation so it boosted the using of standard tools usage in economical analyzing in health car so gradually the relation between economy and health were accepted.

In first years of this decade economists gradually discussed the important case of diseased peoples and proposed appropriate structures for franchise and pricing levels.

Gertler et al in 1987 used a model of demand anticipation which was able to provide the guessed demand anticipation through imperfectness between price and revenue from data collected in Peru. They found out that there is a relation between demands of health care watch and low incomes so the high prices decrease the demand. This survey indicates that increasing diseased share in health costs may decrease the accessibility to health care services in compare to wealthy accessibility to these services.

Because the pricing based on final cost price of health care services without prepayment or diseased partnership is impossible and impropriate , so the health insurance is observed as new revenue resources .In addition the advocates of health care insurance is reasoning that through this system the load of health care costs for staffs who use health care insurance system off take from tax system and the new financial resources can be allocated to poor people (World Bank, 1987).

D. Health Economy Views in 1990

In this decade the quality of health care services was the first priority, the researches about economical condition were widespread which included the priorities of public sector and financial resources allocation, supplying the financial resources, the habits of private sector and habits of consumers.

In this decade the documents of development report of World Bank was recommended the priorities for all private and public sectors.

The first priority of Cost-Effectiveness analyses on politicians, programs and health care systems. It seems that the main content of 1990 researches is about market and competition. And the health institution, habits and change of motivation in organization is scrutinized and emphasized.

Also using some market mechanisms in public sector will boost while the trends of health research and policies may be determined by developed countries which emphasize the importance of essential separation of customers and service providers the competition to attract customers and their satisfaction.

1.7 NEED FOR STUDY

Importance of Insurance

Having health insurance is important because coverage helps people to get timely medical care and improves their lives and health. Some may believe that people always have access to medical care because they can always go to an emergency room. But even areas with well supported safetynet care do not remove barriers to access to the same extent as does having health insurance. "Coverage matters," concluded the Institute of Medicine (IOM) during a recent multiyear appraisal.[11] Indeed, the prestigious IOM estimated that lack of coverage was associated with about 18,000 extra deaths per year among uninsured adults.[12] Several points deserve emphasis.

1. Uninsured people receive less medical care and less timely care

Overall, uninsured people get about half as much care as the privately insured, as measured in dollars spent on their care—even taking into account free care received from providers. This discrepancy holds true even when spending is adjusted for age, income, health status, and other factors. (This finding and most information presented here do not come directly from District sources, for which data are often lacking. But most patterns are believed to generally true of all locations.) Uninsured adults get fewer preventive and screening services and on a less timely basis. Shortfalls are documented for many types of illness or condition, including screening for cervical and breast cancer as well as testing for high blood pressure cholesterol. Cancers, for example, are more likely to be diagnosed at a later stage of illness, when treatment is less successful. Uninsured pregnant women use fewer prenatal services, and uninsured children and adults are less likely than their uninsured counterparts to report having a regular source of care, to see medical providers, or to receive all recommended treatment. Shortfalls are particularly notable for chronic conditions.For instance, uninsured adults with heart conditions are less likely to stay on drug therapy for high blood pressure. Some uninsured people may decide not to obtain insurance precisely because they expect not to need medical care, so simple comparisons of the insured and uninsured can be misleading. However, many studies adjust for factors like age and health status that affect need for care. One recent study examined people who experienced an unintentional injury or a new chronic condition—times when care is more clearly needed. Uninsured individuals were less likely to obtain any medical care, and if they did receive some initial care, they were more likely to get none of the recommended follow-up care.

2. Uninsured people have worse health outcomes

The "bottom line" for uninsured people is that they are sicker and more apt to die prematurely than their insured counterparts. Conversely, having health coverage is associated with better health-related outcomes. Evidence comes from many studies using a variety of data sources and different methods of analysis.[17] Death risk appears to be 25 percent or higher for people with certain chronic conditions, which led to the IOM estimate of some 18,000 extra deaths per year.

Some complain that low health status may be a cause of uninsured status, rather than the other way around. (Note that this objection is the opposite of the complaint noted above that good health may promote uninsurance.) Again, however, as the IOM noted, several studies use statistical methods to adjust for this "reverse causation," and still find that lack of health insurance results in poorer health outcomes. The study of unexpected accidents and new chronic conditions also addressed this issue; its short-term follow-up showed that uninsured accident victims were more likely to have ended treatment without being fully recovered, and that those with chronic conditions still reported worse health status.[18]

3. Lack of insurance is a fiscal burden for uninsured people and their families

Uninsured people do not benefit from the discounted medical prices that are routinely negotiated by private health plans or imposed by public programs. Until recently, those without coverage were billed full hospital charges, for example. The low incomes of some patients qualify them for charity care, but others have often been dunned for unpaid bills. Uninsured families report medical bill problems at double or triple the rate of insured families, and medical bills have been found a contributing factor in a sixth or more of bankruptcies, according to various surveys.[19]

A recent movement to reduce charges for the uninsured has gained strength among public officials and from hospitals, and it may have alleviated this problem. On the other hand, affordability problems have increased along with rapid growth in the costs of care. The IOM noted that low levels of insurance in an area can also burden medical providers because of higher demand for free or reduced-cost care.

4. The benefits of expanding coverage outweigh the costs for added services

Expanding coverage would improve health, lengthen lives, reduce disability, help control communicable diseases, and raise productivity. Newly insured people would get more services, above what they currently pay out of pocket or receive from medical providers in the form of uncompensated care. This can be expected to raise medical spending, but by less than the value of longevity and other benefits achieved.[20] Such estimates are complex to make and do not address political issues concerning the sources for financing increases in spending, especially the likelihood that expansions would shift some spending from the private to the public sector.

5. Safety-net care from hospitals and clinics improves access to care but does not fully substitute for health insurance

Proximity to safety-net hospitals or clinics increases access to care, according to studies using various methodologies.[21] Better access presumably improves health outcomes, although this effect appears less well documented, and safety-net access may provide less continuity of care than insurance. Comparison across states shows that access to care is better where governments and private payers better support the safety net, but that the improvement is less than that insurance achieves.[22] Similarly, communities that have high capacity of community health clinics have better access to care than communities with low capacity, but the effect on access of higher insurance coverage rates is even greater.[23] Insurance likely costs more as well, however, and it can be argued that public budgeting can control public safety-net subsidies, whereas an insurance entitlement like Medicaid is a more open-ended commitment of public resources. Support for safety-net care can be seen as complementary to insurance expansion. Some people will always remain uninsured, and community clinics add capacity to otherwise underserved geographic areas. Clinics may also be better for addressing access problems attributable to cultural and language barriers.

Most benefits of insurance coverage are estimated for coverage in general, not for every type of insurance. Medicaid has sometimes been separately analyzed and achieves less on some measures than do private coverage.[24] One possible reason is that enrollees more often go on and off coverage; another is that Medicaid programs often pay lower rates to participating providers. Private insurance coverage that differs from traditional patterns—for instance, limited-benefit coverages or plans with very high deductibles—might also achieve lesser health improvements. Conversely, adding additional benefits to existing conventional coverage will not necessarily achieve improvements of proportionate magnitude. Insurance and access to safety-net services are far from the only influences on health and longevity.

Environmental and public health measures can have major impacts as well, including promotion of vaccinations, smoking cessation, and maintenance of healthy weight.[25]

1.8 SCOPE OF THE STUDY

The topic is titled "Impact of Health Insurance on Health Care Services in India-A Case Study of Mysore City". This is confined to be a study on the impact on the health insurance on health care service scenario; however, the area of study chosen is that of Mysore City, in Karnataka State. The reason behind this is the fact that Mysore is one of the fast growing Tier II cities in India and has several organisations belonging to the Public and Private Sectors; research Institutes of repute and enjoys the sobriquet as the cultural capital of Karnataka.

Further it was observed that it had all the major types of Hospitals, i.e., Government and Semi Government Hospitals, Corporate Hospitals, Private

Hospitals and Super Specialty Hospitals; which facilitated the study very well. Hence, the researcher selected Mysore city and surrounding areas for his Collection of Data.

This City enjoys a heterogeneous population as the employees of the aforementioned organizations are from all parts of India and are residents here. As a heritage city absorbing all modern amenities particularly health facilities. Though many studies conducted on health, the study related to health insurance is a new attempt which is the need of present context.

1.9 LIMITATIONS OF THE STUDY

As all aspects of health care and wellness cannot be brought under a single study, the limitations are as following:

1. This study has taken the voluntarily insured under the scope and has not taken those who belong to the Government sector or those covered by the employer such as the Railways, etc.

2. This study is mainly aimed at the satisfaction levels of the health insured and is not to suggest which of the insured respondents are better than the others.

3. The study is limited to Mysore City of Karnataka State in India.

4. Due to time constraints and as a foreigner only limited respondents are choosen for collecting opinions.

1.10 RESEARCH OBJECTIVES

1. To study the nature and functioning of health insurance in Indian context

2. To study the influence of various demographic factors of insured on health insurance related issues.

3. To study the opinion of health insured towards health insurance and related aspects.

4. To study the hurdles faced by insured in claiming health insurance.

5. To study the attitude of insured and non insured towards health insurance.

6. To suggest proper measures to improve effective functioning in health insurance sector

1.11 RESEARCH HYPOTHESES

With respect to the objective, following hypotheses were formulated.

H1: Insured respondents vary significantly in their opinion on the health economics regarding health insurance for the following

a. Income

b. Expenditure

c. Amount invested on health insurance

H2: Demographic variables of insured respondents have significant influence over health insurance issues.

H3: Insured respondents vary in their opinion on claiming health insurance and other aspects.

H4: Insured respondents face several hurdles in claiming, documentation related issues.

H5: Insured and non-insured respondents differ significantly in their attitude towards health insurance with special reference to

a. Accessibility

b. Time spent

c. Cost of health care services

1.12 ORGANISATION OF THE STUDY

This study consists of seven chapters with various sections and subsections. Chapter I present the Introduction of the Study. Chapter II presents a Review of Related Literature. Chapter III describes the Methodology of the Study. Chapter IV deals with the Profile of the Study Area. Chapter V deals with the Existing Health Services System. Chapter VI gives the details of Analysis and Interpretation of the Data. Chapter VII contains Findings, Suggestions and Conclusions of the Study.

1.13 SUMMARY

This chapter highlights the importance and conceptual background of health insurance. The chapter also discusses need of the study, research objectives and hypotheses of the study.

The next chapter presents the relevant literature related to the topic of the study and its important variables.

CHAPTER – II

REVIEW OF RELATED LITERATURE

2.1 INTRODUCTION

There is adequate literature on health insurance and health care services in the form of journals, books and reports. Most of them are related to western countries but literature on Indian health insurance is limited.

2.2 VARIOUS STUDIES

Akerlof (1970) and **Rothschild** and **Stiglitz** (1976) reported that the extent of adverse selection or positive selection into insurance has important repercussions for an insurance provider's ability to cover its costs. Standard insurance theory predicts that insurance markets will suffer from adverse selection, which occurs when less healthy people or people who are more risky with their health are more willing to purchase health insurance because they know that the amount they spend on healthcare will be larger than the premium they will pay. Voluntary health insurance cannot be financially sustainable if adverse selection is severe, since only the most costly patients would find it worthwhile to purchase insurance, and premium levels will not be able to cover the high costs of care. On the other hand, another group of people that may buy health insurance are those who are very risk averse with both their health and their finances. These people may buy insurance to protect themselves financially, but may also be very healthy because they take extra care with their health.

The **RAND Health Insurance Experiment** (1974-1982) in the United States is the only randomized experiment examining the effects of health

23

insurance on health to date. This experiment studied almost 4000 people in 2000 families. Some families were randomly assigned to a free care plan while others were assigned one of several plans that required varying co-payments.

Book et al. (1983) reported that for most health outcomes there were no general health benefits from having more complete insurance (i.e. full coverage). Health benefits were found, however, for individuals with poor vision and for persons with elevated blood pressure.

Lohr et al. (1986) and **Manning et al.** (1987) found that those assigned to a cost-sharing plan sought less treatment than those with full coverage.

Fihn and **Wicher** (1988) and **Lurie et al.** (1984, 1986) study insurance impact using the cancellation of some insurance benefits for former U.S. veterans in Seattle and some poor households in Los Angeles. In both cases, health status of the insured was not strongly correlated with the choice by the Seattle VA Medical Center and the state of California, respectively, to withdraw insurance coverage. The authors found that the cancellation of insurance for both groups of people was associated with reduced use of medical care and increases in blood pressure. Several studies have examined the effects of the very large Medicare (for those over 65) and Medicaid (for the poor and near-poor) insurance programs in the United States.

Piper and **Ray** (1990) found no difference in the proportion of women receiving prenatal care in the first trimester immediately before and after Medicaid coverage was expanded in Tennessee. A follow-up study examining a longer period, however, finds a significant improvement in the adequacy of prenatal care.

Keeler (1992) concluded that the improvement in high blood pressure led to a statistically significant 10% reduction in mortality risk, apparently due to increased detection and treatment of high blood pressure among low-income households with free care. Forgone treatment for those with cost-sharing was primarily for preventive visits to doctors and "elective" care such as mental health treatment as opposed to emergency care.

Short and **Lefkowitz** (1992) modeled the probability that preschool children have at least one well-child visit per year. Relative to uninsured children, they find insignificant positive effect of full-year Medicaid and smaller, generally insignificant positive effects for private insurance and partial-year Medicaid coverage. They found that both Medicaid and private insurance are positively and significantly related to the probability of having at least 1 visit related to a specific medical condition during a 12-month period for children living at higher than, but not lower than, 200% FPL. This is similar to the pattern found by **Marquis** and **Long** (1995) for all visits. Similarly, **Currie** and **Thomas** (1995) found that both types of insurance increase the number of "visits for illness" for whites but have no significant effect for blacks. Currie and Thomas (1995) obtained similar results using data from a different source but similar time period. To control for unobserved heterogeneity, they also estimate fixed effect logic models. The fact that the results from these models are quite similar to their OLS results provides support for the validity of simpler econometric specifications in this context. **Currie** and **Gruber** (1996a) have done extensive research on the effects of the Medicaid eligibility expansions of the late 1980s and early 1990s, including a study that focuses on utilization by children. One important difference between their work and most other studies in the literature is that the insurance variable they use is Medicaid eligibility instead of actual coverage. Thus, their "treatment" group includes individuals who were eligible but did not actually have Medicaid coverage, and the comparison group contains not only the uninsured but also people with private coverage. Using 1984-1992 NHTS data, they estimate the effect of Medicaid eligibility on the probability of having at least one physician visit during a 1-year period. Their preferred specification indicates an increase of 10%. **Banthin** and **Selden** (2003) also examined the effect of Medicaid eligibility on the probability of having at least 1 visit. Despite using different data and a different research design, they obtained a very similar result: a 9% effect on the probability of at least one visit.

Spillman (1992), **Hahn** (1994), **Marquis** and **Long** (1994-1995) and **Long**, **Marquis** and **Rodgers** (1998) conducted four studies using different data but a similar research design estimate an effect of private insurance on outpatient utilization ranging from 1 to 2 visits per year Comparisons across these studies suggest that the effect is larger for women than for men and may have grown during the 1980s. Also, full-year measures of insurance tend to indicate a larger effect than point-in-time measures. Another study of low-income women (**Almeida**, **Dubay** and **Ko**, 2001) finds an effect of private insurance that is on the low end of this range-1.1 visits per year-and a larger effect for Medicaid-3 visits per year. This pattern may reflect the differences in cost sharing between Medicaid and the types of private insurance held by low-income women, although unmeasured differences in health status may also be a factor.

Haas (1993) studied the expansion of the Healthy Start program covering low-income pregnant women in Massachusetts and found that increasing program eligibility cut-off from 100-185% of poverty line had no effect on birth outcomes.

Marquis and **Long** (1994) seeks to understand how differences in data sources and econometric specifications affect estimates of the "uninsured access gap" — that is, the additional care that the uninsured would consume if provided with insurance. For children, they examine annual ambulatory contacts using the 1987 National Medical Expenditure Survey (NMES) and several National Health Interview Survey (NHIS) files spanning the years 1984 to 1989. The results from the two data sources are remarkably consistent, implying that privately insured children average one more physician visit per year than uninsured children. This is comparable to the result found by **Spillman** (1992) using earlier data.

Purohit and **Siddiqui** (1994) examined the utilization of health services in India by making the comparison of Indian states in terms of low, medium and high household expenditure on health care and concluded that there is no serious government initiative to encourage utilization of health services by means of devising health insurance.

Stoddard, **St. Peter** and **Newacheck** (1994) examined the relationship between insurance and the probability of any utilization for children who report chronic conditions indicating a need for care. Drawing the sample in this way reduces the potential bias from unobserved heterogeneity, since all children in their sample have a chronic condition, but makes it difficult to generalize to children without these conditions. Because of a small sample, they are unable to distinguish between private and public insurance. Their results indicate that insurance increases utilization by between 21% and 36%.

Marquis and **Long** (1995) find that private insurance increases inpatient utilization by between 0.16 and 0.24 days per year, depending on the survey used. **Hahn's** (1994) results based on the NMES and **Long, Marquis** and **Rodgers** (1998) estimates from the Survey of Income and Program Participation (SIPP) are quite comparable to Marquis and Long's results using the same data sets. Marquis and Long found that the effect of insurance on hospital utilization is larger for adults in fair/poor health than for those reporting good/excellent health, which mirrors their findings for outpatient care. They consider the sensitivity of their results to the way insurance is measured as well as to other modifications in the econometric specifications. These tests provide some information on how insurance effects vary across the population and how their estimates are affected by the inclusion or exclusion of key variables. They find that insurance has a smaller effect for poor children compared to those in families with incomes higher.

Wolfe and **Hill** (1995) concluded that the empirical evidence indicates that workers who are in poorer health are less likely to obtain employer-sponsored coverage (**Buchmueller** 1995; **Stroupe, Kinney** and **Kniesner** 2000; **Blumberg** and **Nichols** 2001; **Holahan** 2001). In contrast, adults with Medicaid coverage tend to have poorer health than the uninsured or privately insured (**Holahan** 2001). This is presumably the case because of the historical link between Medicaid and cash welfare combined with the fact that poor health reduces labor supply and increases welfare participation.

Currie and Gruber (1996) estimated the effect of Medicaid eligibility on the probability that a child is hospitalized during a 1-year period. According to their preferred (IV) model, Medicaid eligibility raises the probability of being hospitalized by 4%, which is comparable to the effect that Spillman (1992) found for private insurance coverage (3%). Currie (2000) found a slightly smaller effect for native-born children and no significant effect for immigrant children.

Sanyal (1996) observed that the burden of health care expenditure in rural areas was twice in 1986-87 as compared to 1963-64 and also provided that household is the main contributor to the financing of health care in India, so the health planners would have to pay more consideration regarding this.

Currie and Gruber (1997) study how the variable timing of the expansion of Medicaid across states affected children and pregnant women. Both groups increased doctor and hospital usage in states where Medicaid was first to expand, as compared to states where the program was enacted later. The authors estimate that increased utilization of care led to a decline of 1.3 deaths per 10,000 children, relative to a baseline mortality rate of 3.1 deaths/10,000 children. They also found an 8.5% decline in the infant mortality rate.

Phelps (1997) expressed that according to standard economic theory, health insurance coverage induces greater medical care utilization by reducing the cost of care to patients. While the normative implications of this "moral hazard" effect are the subject of some debate (Pauly, 1994; Gaynor and Vogt, 1997), the positive prediction that insurance is likely to increase the use of care is well accepted. Obtaining policy-relevant empirical estimates of this effect can, however, be difficult. There are four important methodological considerations that complicate using results from empirical studies to forecast the effect of insurance expansions on medical care utilization. Perhaps the most important is the possibility that estimates of the effect of insurance on utilization may be biased due to self-selection and unobserved heterogeneity, that is, the endogeneity of insurance coverage. Second, the effect of health insurance coverage on utilization may vary across the population. Third, insurance is not a single homogeneous good, and differences in the level and type of insurance will translate into differences in utilization. Fourth, while insurance-related differences in utilization are generally interpreted to represent demand-side responses by patients to the reduction in the cost of care brought about by insurance coverage, capacity constraints may cause physicians to modify their behavior in response to substantial increases in demand. Before reviewing the literature, we discuss each of these methodological concerns.

Ray, Mitchel and **Piper** (1997) gains were largest for demographic groups most likely to have obtained coverage through the expansion, while there was no significant change for women who were unlikely to have been affected. Other state-specific analyses suggest that the Medicaid expansions increased prenatal care use in South Carolina (**Epstein** and **Newhouse**, 1998) and Florida (**Long** and **Marquis**, 1998) where baseline eligibility was low and the safety net is relatively weak, but not in California (**Epstein** and **Newhouse**, 1998), where Medicaid eligibility limits were already high and there are more resources available to uninsured women.

Andaleeb (1998, 2001) proposed and tested a five- factor model that explains considerable variation in customer satisfaction with hospitals. These

30

factors include communication with patients, competence of the staff, their demeanor, quality of the facilities and perceived costs. An examination of the standardized beta values in the regression model used in the study suggests that perceived competence of the hospital staff and their demeanor have the greatest impact on customer satisfaction. These are followed closely in importance by perceived hospital costs. The quality of communication and the general condition of the facilities were also significant but less important in explaining customer satisfaction with hospital services.

Cutler and **Zeckhaus** (1998) find evidence that people with higher expected medical expenditures (measured in a variety of ways across studies) are more likely to buy insurance or pay for health insurance at higher premiums than those with lower expected medical expenditures. However, the extent of adverse selection in health and other insurance is often found to be minimal (**Wolfe** and **Goddeeris**, 1991; **Finkelstein** and **Poterba**, 2004) or non-existent (**Cawley** and **Philipson**, 1999; **Cardon** and **Hendel**, 2001; **Finkelstein** and **McGarry**, 2006). There is also some recent evidence of positive selection into health insurance (**Fang et al.**, 2008).

Lave et al. (1998) examine the change in utilization for children enrolled in state-sponsored programs for low-income children in Pennsylvania and New York. Since the programs are similar to ones created by the State Children's Health Insurance Program (SCHIP), these studies are relevant for understanding the impact of SCHIP programs and future incremental expansions. In their evaluation of two Pennsylvania programs, used a before-and-after research design that compares utilization for the 6 months prior to enrollment with utilization for the first and second 6-month periods after enrollment. Comparing utilization in the first post enrollment period to that of the pre-enrollment period implies that insurance leads to an increase of 0.93 visits per year, which is quite similar to the effects found by **Marquis** and **Long** (1994-1995) and **Spillman** (1992). Results based on the second post enrollment period, however, imply smaller effects.

World Bank (1999), **van Damme et al.** (2004), **Annear et al.** (2006) reported that medical expenditures are consistently cited as a major economic burden for poor Cambodian families and health insurance is, at its core, a product meant to reduce the financial risk of health problems. In addition, descriptive evidence suggests that health insurance really may improve economic outcomes in poor countries. Most of the evidence on the relationship between economic outcomes and insurance status comes from developing countries. With the exception of evidence from China, there tends to be a positive relationship between access to health insurance and good economic outcomes (namely, lower out-of-pocket health expenditures and higher non-medical consumption). This leads us to be hopeful that having SKY insurance will improve economic outcomes for Cambodian families. However, as previously discussed, studies in developing countries to date are largely descriptive rather than causal. By including economic outcomes in the survey, this study will help to establish the firm causal link that is missing in other studies.

Dafny and **Gruber** (2000) examined the effect of the Medicaid expansions on avoidable hospitalizations. Their results imply that Medicaid eligibility reduces the rate of avoidable hospitalizations by 3.4% while increasing the overall hospitalization rate. One interpretation is that by improving access to preventive and primary care for poor children, the Medicaid expansions led to a more efficient use of health care resources. They do several "back-of-the-envelope" calculations that suggest that the cost savings from reducing avoidable hospitalizations more than offset the cost of additional physician visits generated by expanding Medicaid. Work by **Kaestner et al.** (**Kaestner, Racine** and **Joyce** 2000; **Kaestner, Joyce** and **Racine,** 2001) provides mixed results on the question of whether expanding insurance coverage would reduce avoidable hospitalizations.

Gumber and **Kulkarni** (2000) undertaken a case study in Gujarat and provided that SEWA a type of health insurance scheme is strongly preferred by those who can't afford and also not access the services of various other schemes.

Holl et al. (2000) analyses New York's Child Health Plus program (CHPlus) finds larger effects than the cross-sectional studies, although this difference may be explained by the way the data were collected. Preprogram data came from retrospective chart review, whereas post enrollment utilization was measured sing parent interviews. To the extent that the chart review data are incomplete, preprogram utilization will be underestimated causing changes in utilization to be overstated. The difference in the completeness of the two data sources is a likely explanation for the finding that utilization was found to increase by between 0.6 and 1.6 visits per year for previously insured children. If we assume that these changes for continuously enrolled children can be entirely attributed to measurement error, the "true" effect of CHPlus for uninsured children is between 0.83 and 1.29 visits per year, which is consistent with the estimates mentioned above. This suggests that estimates based on cross-sectional differences between children with and without insurance are good estimates of the effect of change in utilization associated with extending coverage to uninsured children.

Ambuj Bharadwaj et al. (2001) estimate that the private sector Hospitals have come up to provide the health care in a large way and this sector shares a major part of GDP 4.7% compared to 1.2% of public sector. 78.4% of total expenditure on health is shared by private sector, while 20% is accounted for by public sector.

McGee and **Cegala** (2001) face-to-face trained patients to ask questions for the physician to be clearer or more specific in the three phases of medical consultation: history taking, examination and conclusion. Patients were also told that they were there not only to provide information for their physician but also to seek information from their physician. It was found that trained patients showed a significant increase in overall participation, overall question asking and requests for clarification and information recall. This includes overall satisfaction, relationship satisfaction, communication satisfaction and expertise satisfaction. No consistent gender differences were found in patient satisfaction.

McKinley R.K. et al. (2001) have speculated that patient expectation of care they receive has an important impact on satisfaction of patients with inappropriately high expectations may be dissatisfied with optimal care and those with inappropriately low expectations may be satisfied with deficient care.

Narayanan Devadasan, Bart Criel, Wim Van Damme, Kent Ranson and **Patrick Almeida, Dubay** and **Ko** (2001) concluded that study of low-income women finds an effect of private insurance that is on the low end of this range 1.1 visits per year-and a larger effect for Medicaid 3 visits per year. This pattern may reflect the differences in cost sharing between Medicaid and the types of private insurance held by low-income.

Prasanta Mahapatra et al. (2001) have identified in their work that, Corruption by all categories of staff was the greatest cause for dissatisfaction, followed by general cleanliness, poor utilities etc. Also significantly high level of dissatisfaction was noted regarding patient's assessment of technical quality of doctor's work and less time spent by the doctor with the patients, which are the main causes for people to go for private healthcare organizations, where majority of patients who come for treatment to public hospital are poor and illiterate.

Yip and **Berman** (2001) and **Jutting** (2004) in their studies they find a positive relationship between insurance coverage and health-care utilization and quality of care (**Dong et al.**, 1999; **Wagstaff et al.**, 2007). Results are more mixed regarding the relationship between insurance status and health expenditures.

Case et al. (2002), **Currie et al.** (2003) and **Smith** (2005) concluded recent theoretical work has focused on how the problem of adverse selection may be mitigated by factors such as wealth (which could both increase the probability of insurance purchase and improve health outcomes), risk aversion (which could increase the probability of insurance purchase and decrease the amount of risk one takes with one's health) (**Jullien et al.**, 2003; **Chiappori et al.**, 2004) or optimism (where some people underestimate their accident probability, and thus don't buy insurance, but are also less willing to take precautions, leading to a higher probability of a health shock) (**Koufopoulus**, 2005).

Gertler and **Gruber** (2002), **Wagstaff** and **Doorslaer** (2003) and **Gertler, Levine** and **Moretti** (2003) reported that when a person experiences a bad shock to health, their medical expenses typically rise and their contribution to household income and home production (e.g. cooking or childcare) declines.

Lichtenberg (2002) and **Card, Dobkin** and **Maestas** (2007) studied the effect of Medicare by comparing health and health care outcomes of people just below 65 (many of whom lack health insurance) to outcomes of those just over 65 (all of whom are covered by Medicare). Both papers found that the group with more insurance received more care and had better health outcomes (although the reductions in mortality were often not statistically significant in the **Card et al.** study).

Michael Kent Ranson (2002) reported that in India, as in many other developing countries, spending related to hospitalization is often catastrophic for household finances. His study shows that community-based health insurance schemes can effectively protect poor households from the uncertain risk of medical expenses, and they can be implemented in areas where institutional capacity is too weak to organize mandatory, nationwide risk-pooling. The study identified various aspects of scheme design and management that can be tailored (depending on the priorities of scheme administrators) to achieve such goals as risk-sharing, cross-subsidization, financial protection of households and scheme financial viability. Firstly, this study suggests that community-based health insurance schemes can include poor people, including people and households below the poverty line. Factors that may facilitate inclusion of the poor include an affordable premium, external assistance and nesting the scheme within a larger organization that addresses other needs of the poor (for example, providing access to credit, education and bargaining power in the workplace). Secondly, the

36

financial risk borne by a scheme can be limited by placing a cap on the benefits provided. However, this also limits the extent of risk-pooling and cross-subsidization provided by the scheme. There will inevitably be cases where hospital expenditures far exceed this cap, with dire financial consequences for the insured. Thirdly, in order to relieve the financial burden of expenditures on households, reimbursement under a scheme should be fast and easy. This needs administration of the scheme, particularly processing of claims, to happen as close to claimants as possible. Fourthly, to tine-tune the design of a scheme needs information on who is enrolled and excluded, rates and causes of hospitalization, expenditure on hospitalization, and barriers that prevent enrolment in the scheme and use of the scheme by the insured. A system for monitoring and evaluating the scheme is vital. However, every change that administrators make to the fund - whether an increase in breadth or amount of the benefits package or interventions to improve rates and timeliness of insurance claim submission - will have to be weighed against impact on the fund's affordability and ability to recover costs.

Reyaz Ahmed et al. (2002) have found that outpatient services in a Teaching Hospital in Jammu and Kashmir are being utilised by married adult males who are rural, illiterates and of poor socio economic status.

Asfaw (2003) concluded that rigorous evidence on the impact of insurance is scarce, and there are even fewer studies on the effects of insurance in developing countries. One reason for the lack of evidence is that it is difficult to find a valid control group for the insured. We cannot simply compare the outcomes of insured and uninsured households, since health insurance status is typically strongly correlated with other household characteristics. For example, rich and well educated households typically have both better health and better health insurance coverage (**Cameron** and **Trivedi**, 1991; **Jütting**, 2004), but the positive correlation between health and insurance status tells us nothing about the impact of insurance. On the other hand, those in poor health may be more likely to pay for health insurance (**Ellis**, 1989; **Cutler** and **Reber**, 1998), but finding that the insured tend to be sicker would not imply that insurance causes illness.

Han et al. (2003) found on all four dimensions of patient satisfaction i.e. overall satisfaction, relationship satisfaction, communication satisfaction and expertise satisfaction, patients who received training, have scored significantly higher and were more satisfied than patients who received no training. No consistent gender differences were found in patient satisfaction in both experimental and control groups.

Jowett et al. (2003) and **Jütting** (2004) find a negative relationship between insurance coverage and health expenditures in Vietnam, and **Yip** and **Berman** (2001) in Egypt. But some find that out-of-pocket spending is the same or even higher for the insured when compared to the uninsured (**Wagstaff et al.**, 2007a and **Wagstaff et al.**, 2007b) in their studies of China. These authors explain this surprising finding as being a result of the institutional structure of health-care in China, which favors increased utilization and substitution toward more expensive services and treatments.

Kim et al. (2003) initiated a program called "smart patient coaching" in which a part of the training consisted of instructing patients to ask the provider for clarification when the patient did not understand something during the consultation. It was found that trained patients asked more overall questions, expressed more concerns but did not ask more clarifying questions in comparison with the untrained group.

Talluru Sreenivas et al. (2003) evaluate patient satisfaction as a vital tool to measure efficiency of Government, Quasi Government and Corporate sector hospitals. One of the hospitals managed by corporate sector was found to be satisfying the needs of patients commendably. Patient's satisfaction is one of the established yardsticks to measure success of the services.

Wagstaff and **Pradhan** (2003) overcome some of the selection bias plaguing most studies in their study of Vietnam's health insurance (VHI) program. This program was much more likely to cover those enrolled in high school or college or those working for the government or state-owned employers. To reduce selection bias, the authors "match" insured households to uninsured households with similar characteristics, and compare outcomes of the insured to those of the uninsured with similar profiles. They also use a double-difference estimator, comparing the *change* in outcomes over time between the insured and uninsured. This technique reduces selection bias since it does not assume that insured and uninsured households are identical on unobservable characteristics. However, as the authors note, their study still must assume that in the absence of insurance, *changes* in outcomes over the study period would have been the same for the insured and the uninsured, an assumption which may not hold. With this possible bias in mind, the authors find positive impacts of insurance. In the insured group, children grew more rapidly and adults had improved BMI (body mass index) scores. The authors also find that the probability of contact with health care providers was higher, out-of-pocket health expenditures were lower, and non-medical household consumption was higher among the insured group. Though a firm causal relationship between insurance status and outcomes has yet to be established, many studies do present interesting evidence on the correlation between insurance status and outcomes. In all of these studies the relationship tends to vary across income deciles.

Ahuja and **De** (2004) confirmed that the demand for health insurance is limited where supplies of health services is weak and explained interstate variation in demand for health insurance by poor in relation to variation in healthcare infrastructure. Beside this the study also provided that healthcare infrastructure is positively related to demand for health insurance by poor, whereas the proportion of Below Poverty Line (BPL) population is negatively related. In order to build demand for health insurance, it is necessary to address the demand side and at the same time design the insurance schemes by taking into consideration the paying capacity of the poor.

Asgary, **Willis**, **Taghvari** and **Refeian** (2004) estimated the demand and willingness to pay for health insurance by rural households in Iran and concluded that a significant percentage of population (more than 38%) live in rural areas, but the health care insurance currently operating in urban areas.

Boshoff and **Gray** (2004) investigated the relationship between service quality, customer satisfaction, and loyalty (as measured by purchasing intentions) among patients in the private healthcare industry in South Africa, revealed that the service quality dimensions of nursing staff empathy, assurance and tangibles impact positively on patient's loyalty.

Harrington et al. (2004) found that patients who received communication skill training, regardless of the type of training showed a consistent increase in requests for clarification. They argued that patients might feel more comfortable to ask questions for clarification than to initiate questions of their own. Clarifying questions are based on the content of the on-going conversation, thus perceived as appropriate for patients to ask.

Henry J. Kaiser (2004) stated that medicaid is the nation's major public health program for low-income Americans, financing health and long-term care services for more than 50 million people – a source of health insurance for 38 million low-income children and parents and a critical source of acute and long-term care coverage for 12 million elderly and disabled individuals, including more than 6 million low-income Medicare beneficiaries. Medicaid accounts for 17 percent of all personal health care spending, finances 17 percent of hospital care, 12 percent of physician and other professional services, 17 percent of prescription drug spending, and nearly half of all nursing home care.

Philip Kotler (2004) has explained that customer's expectations are the true standards for judging service quality understanding the nature and determinants are essential to ensure that service performance meets or exceeds expectations. If a hospital raises expectations too high, the patient is likely to be disappointed. However if the hospitals set expectations too low, it won't attract enough patients.

Richard B. Saltman, **Reinhard Busse** and **Josef Figueras** (2004) elaborate information on social health insurance (SHI). In this book chapter I entitled concepts of social health insurance. The concept of social health insurance

(SHI) is deeply ingrained in the fabric of health care systems in Western Europe. It provides the organizing principle and a preponderance of the funding in seven countries - Austria, Belgium, France, Germany, Luxembourg, the Netherlands and Switzerland. Since 1995, it has also become the legal basis for organizing health services in Israel. Previously, SHI models played an important role in a number of other countries that subsequently changed to predominantly tax-funded arrangements in the second half of the twentieth century – Denmark (1973), Italy (1978), Portugal (1979), Greece (1983) and Spain (1986). These multiple imperatives are captured in the SHI pyramid presented in the figure. In this conceptual approach, the lowest level serves as the essential foundation from which higher levels draw their character and legitimacy, and upon which these higher levels are thus integrally dependent. As his Figure suggests, the base of the four-part SHI pyramid incorporates the national culture and historically-tied values found in the broad society. The second level - dependent on society but functioning independently - is the nation state, which constructs the legislative, regulatory and judicial arrangements for SHI systems. Built on these two lower levels are, at the third level of the pyramid, the actual organizational and administrative arrangements of each studied country's SHI system. Lastly and therefore most contingent upon and least independent of the lower three levels of the pyramid - one finds issues of funding. Thus, discussions and analyses that focus exclusively on the funding level alone implicitly assume the existing configuration and activities of the three lower levels.

van Damme et al. (2004); **Annear et al.** (2006); **Factsheet N.** (2007) reiterates that according to the WHO, "Each year, approximately 150 million people experience *financial catastrophe*, meaning they are obliged to spend on health care more than 40% of the income available to them after meeting their basic needs." Low income and high medical expenses can also lead to debt, sale of assets, and removal of children from school, especially in poor nations. A short-term health shock can thus contribute to long-term poverty.

Zebiene et al. (2004) studied the relationship between meeting patient's expectations and patient's satisfaction with medical consultations in Lithuania. Analysis of 460 sets of questionnaires revealed that satisfaction with medical consultations was higher among patients who have a greater number of expectations met. The study found that physician's success in meeting different types of patient expectations have different influences on patient satisfaction. The most important expectations to be met were "understanding and explanation" followed by expectations of "emotional support".

Ahuja and **Narang** (2005) provided an overview of existing forms and emerging trends in health insurance for low income segment in India and concluded that health insurance schemes have considerable scope of improvement for a country like India by providing appropriate incentives and bringing these under the regulatory ambit. The study suggested that in order to develop health insurance for poor in a big way, health care provisions need to be strengthened and streamlined as well as coordination among multiple agencies is needed.

Finkelstein and **McKnight** (2005) find that health care utilization increased fastest in areas where Medicare caused the largest increase in health insurance coverage. They do not find such areas experienced a faster decline in mortality.

Hanratty (2005) compares health outcomes across Canadian provinces that were early adopters of universal health insurance (1962) to outcomes in provinces that were later adopters (up to 1972). Her results suggest that there was a significant reduction of 4% in the infant mortality rate as a result of this government health insurance program and a smaller reduction in low birth weight of about 1.3%.

Jabnoun and **Al-Rasasi** (2005) investigated the relationship between transformational leadership and service quality in the DAE hospitals. Data collected from 242 patients and 201 hospital employees showed that UAE patients were generally satisfied with the quality of service provided to them by hospitals.

The study found also that service quality is positively related to all dimensions of transformational leadership.

van der Reis and **Xiao** (2005) stated that the factor that is important in the changes that have taken place during the past half century and impact access to medical care is the changed gender ratio of physicians. Today most medical schools have a larger percentage of female than of male students. This changed ratio affects access to care in a negative manner. According to a survey study by **van der Reis** and **Xiao** (2005), 35 percent of USA female physicians work part time. This situation affects the supply shortage of physicians in a negative manner, and an ominous trend in terms of access.

World Health Assembly (2005) reported reveals that health spending through out-of-pocket payment (OOP) is not always easy to cope with. Households may encounter financial hardship and poverty as a result. In fact, over 150 million people face catastrophic health expenditure every year and 100 million fall into poverty worldwide after paying for health care. Thus, benefiting from health care remains difficult or impossible for many households because of financial barriers. Universal coverage and access to health insurance, with an important degree of prepayment, is an important policy objective that could improve financial protection for many. There are different strategies for increasing prepayment and reaching universal coverage. Tax-based systems, social health insurance systems or mixed systems commonly exist in most developed countries which have reached universal coverage. However, for developing countries, transition strategies are usually needed. These strategies include different prepayment mechanisms to reduce OOP and improve access to care, such

45

as mutual health insurance (MHI). However, MHI has often been small scale. Its sustainability and financial risk pooling capacities are considered limited when compared to nationwide schemes. Nonetheless, it can be a first step towards universal coverage for certain countries. In fact, a few countries such as Rwanda, have now managed to scale up MHI. This paper contributes to the evidence on MHI by examining and its effect on utilization and financial risk protection at the national level by analysing survey data from Rwanda.

Bellemare and **Shearer** (2006); **Harrison et al.** (2007); **Anderson** and **Mellor** (2008) reported that one cannot ask people directly the value of their risk aversion or discount rate, questions on risk aversion and discounting are particularly challenging. Risk aversion and discount rates are often measured using games and questions with real money prizes and consequences. However, a less costly alternative is to rely on hypothetical questions in the survey. It is important to learn from experimental work studying the predictive power of these types of hypothetical questions. Often-used measures of risk aversion include hypothetical lotteries and questions asking whether people engage in behavior that is risky for one's physical or financial well-being. Shostack views service as fulfilling certain wants and needs, Services are those separately identifiable, essentially intangible activities, which provide want satisfaction and are not necessarily tied to the sale of a product or another service. To produce a service mayor may not require the use of tangible goods. However when such use is required there is no transfer of title (permanent ownership) to these tangible goods.

Dror (2006) laid seven myths regarding health insurance and examined the realities behind these myths. The evidence shown that most people are willing to pay 1.35% of income or more for health insurance and the solvent market for health insurance business exist in India; however tapping of it is contingent upon understanding the customer's needs and wants.

IRDA Journal (2006) and **IRDA Annual Report** (2006-2007) reported the insurance industry in India registered real growth (measured by first-year premiums) of 94.96 percent, exceeding the growth of 47.94 percent achieved in 2005-2006. The impressive growth has also resulted in greater insurance penetration: insurance penetration, or premium volume, as a ratio of GDP for 2006 was at 4.1 percent for life insurance and 0.6 percent for non-life insurance. The total premium for life and non-life insurance market in India was Rs. 181971.61 crore, or $41.74 billion.

Salgo (2006) conducting health care strictly as a business deteriorates doctor-patient relationship by treating patients like "customers". The unique relationship between patient and physician, fundamental for the practice of good medicine, cannot be equated with the purchase of material goods. The deterioration of the doctor-patient relationship, primarily the result of economic demands from fiscal intermediaries, has clearly had a negative impact on access. Hospitals have made inroads in the practice of medicine through contractual agreements with individual and groups of physicians. For all practical purposes these agreements are commercial contracts subject to the conditions contained in the contract. When financial concern becomes one of major objects of hospitals, there is a shift in attitude within the profession.

Sumninder Kaur Bawa (2006) in his study Health Insurance: An Empirical Study with Reference to Punjab India concluded that the health insurance is not a new concept and the people are also getting aware about it, which mainly comes from TV followed by newspaper, agents, friends, etc., but this awareness has not yet reached the level of subscription. As the results shown that just 19.4% are being covered by some form of health insurance and large chunk of the population is still financing health care expenditure without health insurance. Moreover it was observed that there are 7 key factors by clubbing the related variables under it which are acting as barrier in the subscription of health insurance. These are Lack of Funds to Meet Costly Affair; Lack of Awareness and Willingness to join; Lack of Intermediaries' Outreach and Capabilities; Lack of Reliability and Comprehensive Coverage; Lack of Availability and Accessibility of Services; Narrow Policy Options; and Prefer Other Mode to Invest (followed by friends, relatives, etc.). Alternatively, the analysis of willingness to join and pay for health insurance has been made to know whether non health insurance policyholders are ready to buy it or not and the results provided that very few percentage i.e. 11.9% are ready to buy health insurance without any conditions and 19.8% are willing to buy only if certain conditions will fulfill. Remaining is not ready to buy, still need some time or not provided with any response. As far as the ranking of conditions of buying are concerned, 1 rank is assigned to "if comprehensive coverage provided with least cost" as its weighted average score is 3.36 is more as compared with all other conditions. Whereas 2 rank is assigned to "if some contribution will employer made", followed by "If available with least formalities", "If friends and relatives buy", "If someone suggest about it". Besides this the association between the various variables linked with the respondents has been determined with their willingness to pay for health insurance and the results

48

provided that on the one hand significant association exist between the gender; age; education; occupation; income of respondents with their willingness to pay for health Insurance. On the other hand no significant association exists between the marital status of the respondents with their willingness to pay for health insurance.

Cegala et al. (2007) administered a 14-page booklet instructing patients to provide, seek and verify information in the medical consultation. The information verifying section was designed to train patients to check understanding by asking the physician to repeat or clarify what the physician had just said. To facilitate the learning process, patients were also offered examples. It was found that trained patients asked more questions to verify what was said and their questions were more sophisticated in comparison with untrained patients.

Dror (2007) examined why the "one-size-fits-all" health insurance products are not suitable to low income people in India and provided that there is presence of considerable variability to pay for health insurance which is because of multiple reasons like variability in income, frequency of illness among households, quality and proximity of providers (private, public) in different locations.

van der Stuyft (2007) concluded that CHE (Catastrophic Health Expenditure) is a major cause of impoverishment and patients need to be protected from it. Some of the documented determinants of CHE are poverty. Household size, high medical costs, incidence of illness, payment mechanisms, low benefit packages and presence of 'smokers or drinkers' in the household. They showed that the incidence of CRE is also related to the type of provider; private-for-profit providers considerably increase the probability of CHE. We have documented some of the illnesses that can lead to CHE, namely surgical ailments and admissions for non-communicable diseases. Indian CHI (Community Health Insurance) schemes are able to protect their members against CHE, but only to a limited level. However, this protection can be further enhanced if some design changes are incorporated. To begin with, the upper limit of the benefit package needs to be raised. To keep the premiums affordable, donors or the government would need to directly subsidies the premium, especially for the poorer sections of society. Exclusions need to be minimized to protect vulnerable populations. And finally, scheme managers need to negotiate costs with providers from the start to ensure that costs are contained. Such measures could considerably reduce the incidence and magnitude of CHE and protect households from iatrogenic poverty.

Wagstaff et al. (2007) concluded that non-experimental studies from developing countries sometimes find enrollment to be more common in households with chronically sick members, evidence of adverse selection and commonly find higher enrollment rates in wealthier households, potentially leading to positive selection if wealthier people also tend to be healthier.

Joglekar (2008) examined the impact of health insurance on catastrophic out-of-pocket (OOP) health expenditure in India and taken zero percent as threshold level to define and examine such impact. It showed that in India, OOP health expenditure by households account for around 70% of total expenditure on health and thereby pushes households in to poverty.

Garg and **Karan** (2009) assessed the differential impact of out-of-pocket (OOP) expenditure and its components between developed and less developed regions in India. The results showed that OOP expenditure is about 5% of total households' expenditure (ranging from about 2% in Assam to 7% in Kerala) with higher proportion in rural areas. Further in order to reduce OOP expenditure targeted policies are needed which in turn could help to prevent almost 60% of poverty.

Sona Bedi et al. (2009) identify that if any hospital fulfils patient's expectations, patients are more likely to stay with that particular service provider for a longer time. Patient satisfaction is also the desired outcome of any hospital.

Priyanka Saksena, Adelio Fernandes Antunes, Ke XuLaurent Musango and **Guy Carrin** (2010) in their results find that many households in Rwanda did not seek care when needed and while others were pushed into financial hardship as a result of seeking care. These effects are particularly accentuated for the poor and the uninsured. Indeed, MHI coverage was strongly associated with a reduction in unmet need and risk of catastrophic expenditure. Nonetheless, the MHT benefit package may require some further enhancement. Longer-term financial sustainability of the scheme also needs to be considered in light of this and innovative ways to raise further resources may be needed. Continued expansion of MHI, as supported by these results, may also require further organizational strengthening to ensure that gains from it are maximized.

CHAPTER – III

METHODOLOGY OF THE STUDY

3.1 INTRODUCTION

The successful outcome of any study or research is entirely dependent upon the methodology used. A thoroughly planned approach at the problem in question makes it a systematic and detailed study. The planning and the research design are vital at every stage of the research. This chapter depicts the various aspects that have been considered in the design of this study. It contains the field or the area in which the investigation were undertaken, the tools and the techniques of the study, the modes of their usage and finally in the subsequent chapters, the analysis and conclusions drawn from it are the issues that have been explicitly brought forth, in this chapter.

3.2 SAMPLE OF THE STUDY

A total of 400 respondents belonging to various age groups were chosen through stratified random Sampling Technique, out of 400 respondents, 200 were insured and the other 200 were non-insured. They were contacted personally in ten selected hospitals, with prior information to the concerned authorities of those particular hospitals. All the ten hospitals were located in the city of Mysore. The criteria for the selection of these hospitals were that all of them were having 100 beds or more, multi-speciality hospitals.

In the pretext the respondents were handed the two questionnaire based on their Insurance status. If the respondent had a health insurance he/she was handed with questionnaire which had specific set questions related to those who had health Insurance policy and the other questionnaire was handed to the person who did not have health insurances, which had specific set.

3.2.1 Sampling Technique

The technique used for the sampling is stratified sampling. Further based upon the size, a random size has been arrived at from the subpopulation. The sample size for the present study was calculated using online sample size calculator provided by 'Creative Research Systems' in their website 'http://www.surveysystem.com/sscalc.htm'.

Sample Size Calculator is presented as a public service of Creative Research Systems survey software. One can use it to determine how many people one needs to interview in order to get results that reflect the target population as precisely as needed. One can also find the level of precision you have in an existing sample.

Roughly more than 2,00,000 individuals in and around Mysore city are covered under health insurance either by private agencies or by the government. For a population of 2,00,000 with 5% of the confidence interval and 95% of confidence level, the required minimum sample size was 383. However, the researcher has taken 400 in total as sample for the study.

3.3 TOOLS USED IN THE STUDY

3.3.1 Preparation of the Tools

Two questionnaires were prepared meeting the study subject in mind; one was addressed to the responded who had health insurance and the other to respondents who didn't had any kind of health insurance. Both the questionnaires were tagged with a header stating that all the information collected will be confidential and will not be discussed and further will be only be used for research purpose.

3.3.2 Questionnaire for Insured Respondents

This questionnaire consisted about five parts; the first part dealt with personal information or demographic information of the individual respondents where the respondents were asked about their age, sex, education/qualification, annual income of the respondent.

The second part handled the respondent's background regarding his awareness of health insurance and as such queries.

The third part was about the respondent's health insurance policies and information about their benefits.

The fourth part dealt with respondent's medical expenditure, their feedback on aspects dealing with difficulties of reclaiming and as such. It also contains the availability of insurance, treatment issues and time spending to obtain claims.

The fifth part dealt is an open ended question. Here, the respondents were asked to give opinion in their own words. This part is titled as suggestions.

In whole the questionnaire consisted of 58 questions closed and one open ended Question. Out of the 58 questions, 33 were common with the questions asked to the uninsured also.

The questionnaire was validated by few experts in the academic and educational field.

3.3.3 Questionnaire for Non-Insured Respondents

This questionnaire consisted of 35 questions, the initial questions dealt with personal information such as age, sex, annual income where more of demographic information was elicited in this part.

The other part of the questionnaire elicited responses on health related queries such as respondent's medical history, individual respondent's critical area in emergency situation where he/she feels more difficult and individual's medical expenditures per annum. This questionnaire too as in Insured Questionnaire had all the other general queries.

Fifteen questions for both the insured and the uninsured were used to compare and correlate between the availability of medical care, cost, treatment quality issues and time spending. There were more questions (06) in the insured questionnaire than in the uninsured questionnaire for the above parameters. The uninsured questionnaire, thus had only two questions which were individual than in the insured questionnaire. Therefore the total number of questions is 33.

Both the questionnaires are enclosed as Appendices I and II.

3.4 DATA COLLECTION METHOD

The data collection method is one of utmost steps of research. Hence, the data collection method includes using the existing data through questionnaire.

In present research the data collection methods are both by bibliotheca and field.

In bibliotheca data collection method, the investigation of research literature and other studies is done in libraries and referring to books and articles.

In the field of this research the data collection are carried out through questionnaires which are designed for this purpose.

3.4.1 Procedure

The procedure in this study has been that of conducting a pilot study and based upon its outcome, the main study has been made.

3.4.2 Pilot Study

A pilot study was conducted on a small sample of 10 respondents among them 5 were insured and remaining 5 were non insured respondents. This was conducted to test the feasibility of the tools used. The purpose of the pilot study was:

a. To check the clarity of the items enlisted in the selected questionnaires.

b. To get an approximation of time required to complete the questionnaire.

c. To ensure the feasibility of the tools selected for the study.

d. To have a fair idea of the respondents reaction towards research study and questionnaires.

The following observations were made during the pilot study

1. Most of the respondents expressed their desire to respond to the various test in the local language i.e., in Kannada. Hence the investigator decided to translate all the items on the tests into Kannada by the services of an interpreter.

2. Since the data collection was done on a small sample the instructions were given to each individual separately.

3. Some respondents wanted some feedback about the test results and some guidelines which were incorporated in the main study.

3.4.3 Main Study

As per the researcher's need, an introduction letter was obtained from the Institute of Development Studies, Mysore, so that the hospitals and respondents could recognize me and address me as a research scholar of the department. Then the researcher interacted with the management of ten hospitals in the city of Mysore; subsequently the researcher, with appropriate permission and authorization visited different sections of the hospitals and interviewed their patients. The patients were met and were introduced formally and a good rapport was established by making them understand the need and purpose of the study, so that the patients can answer with at most ease and comfort. If the respondent faced any difficulty in grasping the language or the questions, an immediate assistance was provided to assist the respondent by helping him understand the questions in their regional or understandable language.

Once the data were collected, they were checked for completeness, and a master chart was prepared and fed to the computer using SPSS 16.0 for Windows.

3.5 STATISTICAL METHODS APPLIED

3.5.1 Descriptive Statistics

The Descriptive procedure displays univariate summary statistics for several variables in a single table and calculates standardized values (z scores). Variables can be ordered by the size of their mean (in ascending or descending order), alphabetically, or by the order in which the researcher specifies.

3.5.2 Frequencies

The Frequencies procedure provides statistics and graphical displays that are useful for describing many types of variables. In the present study, frequencies and percentages were calculated for the responses collected from health insured and non-insured respondents.

3.5.3 Chi-Square Test

The Chi-Square Test procedure tabulates a variable into categories and computes a chi-square statistic. This goodness-of-fit test compares the observed and expected frequencies in each category to test either that all categories contain the same proportion of values or that each category contains a user-specified proportion of values. In the present study, Chi-square test was applied to find out the significance of differences between groups of frequencies of responses.

3.5.4 Contingency Coefficient Analysis

The Crosstabs procedure forms two-way and multi-way tables and provides a variety of tests and measures of association for two-way tables. The structure of the table and whether categories are ordered determine what test or measure to use. Contingency coefficient analysis was employed in the present study. In the present study Contingency coefficient test was applied to find out the association between independent variables employed and the responses of the sample studied. All the statistical methods were carried out through the SPSS for Windows (version 16.0).

3.6 LIMITATIONS

The first of the limitations of this study is the fact that the study was made in Mysore City, it cannot be universally applicable as the findings for all over India or elsewhere. This is due to various factors such as the culture, economy and other social considerations.

The barrier which the researcher faced is mainly communication. The researcher had to use the services of an interpreter for the same and was successful in obtaining the necessary information.

Despite of the fact that there are 64 hospitals in Mysore City which provided treatment under the Health Insurance Schemes of both the Government and the private players, only ten of them provided with all the necessary information. The others either provided with only partial information or did not cooperate at all.

Some of the respondents were reluctant to provide with information regarding their personal income. Hence the income parameter is approximately taken as such.

Some of the insurance companies through their representatives also did not permit the respondents to respond freely initially. As it was an academic work, they cooperated eventually.

3.7 ETHICAL ISSUES

1. Written informed consent was obtained from each respondent participating in the study.

2. It was made sure that none felt offended when addressed with questionnaire rendering personal information.

3. All the questions were made sure to be un-prejudiced in all the domains of the two questionnaires.

4. Confidentiality was assured and maintained.

5. The subjects were explained about the nature of study and informed that participation in the study is voluntary and they have the right to opt out at any time.

CHAPTER – IV

PROFILE OF THE STUDY AREA

4.1 INTRODUCTION

Mysore is the second-largest city in the state of Karnataka, India, located at the base of the Chamundi Hills about 146 km (91 miles) southwest of the state capital Bangalore. Population of Mysore City is 3001127 (census 2011). The total City Population at present is 9,83,893. It is the Second biggest city area in terms of Population. Mysore City Corporation (MUDA) is responsible for the civic administration of the city, which is also in the headquarters of the Mysore City and the Mysore division.

Until 1947, Mysore served as the capital of the Kingdom of Mysore. The kingdom was ruled by the Wodeyar dynasty, except for a brief and illustrious period in the late 18th century.

Mysore has 65 wards, in 128.42 in sq Km, It contain 62 Notified slums and 19 un notified slums.

The gender ratio of the city is 1000 females to every 1000 males and the population density is 6,910.5 per square kilometre (17,898 /sq mi). According to the census of 2001, 76.8% of the population is Hindus, 19% are Muslims, 2.8% are Christians, and the remainder belongs to other religions.

Some of the Key demographic features in state are shown in the following table.

Table 4.1: Demographic Profile

Total Population of city (in lakhs)	983893
Slum Population (in lakhs)	167879
Slum Population as percentage of city population	17%
Number of Notified Slums	62
Number of slums not notified	19
Number of Slum Households	20012
Number of slums covered under slum improvement programme (BSUP, IDSMT, etc.)	NA
Number of slums where households have individual water connections	31(all slums)
Number of slums connected to sewerage network*	NA
Number of slums having a Primary school	25
Number of slums having AWC	93
Number of slums having primary health care facility	20

Mysore is located at 12.30°N 76.65°E and has an average altitude of 770 metres (2,526 ft). It is spread across an area of 128.42 km^2 (50 sq mi) at the base of the Chamundi Hills in the southern region of Karnataka. It has several lakes, such as the Kukkarahalli, the Karanji and the Lingambudhi lakes. In 2001, total land area usage in Mysore city was 39.9% residential, 16.1% roads, 13.74% parks and open spaces, 13.48% industrial, 8.96% public property, 3.02% commercial, 2.27% agriculture and 2.02 water. The city is located between two rivers: the Kaveri River flows through the north of the city and the Kabini River, a tributary of the Kaveri, lies to the south. Though Mysore is situated in the relatively safe seismic zone 2 of the earthquake hazard zoning of India, earthquakes of magnitude greater than 4.5 on the Richter scale have been recorded in the vicinity of the city.

Climate

Mysore has a semi-arid climate designated under the Köppen climate classification. The main seasons are summer from March to June, the monsoon season from July to November and winter from December to February. The highest temperature recorded in Mysore was 38.5°C (101°F) on 4th May 2006, and the lowest was 7.7°C (46°F) on 16th January 2012. The city's average annual rainfall is 804.2 mm (31.7 in).

Demographics

According to the provisional results of the 2011 census of India, Mysore had a population of 887,446, consisting of 443,813 males and 443,633 females, The total Population of Urban Agglomeration (U/A) is 9,83,893 making it the second most populous city in Karnataka. The gender ratio of the city is 1000 females to every 1000 males and the population density is 6,910.5 per square kilometre (17,898 /sq mi). According to the census of 2001, 76.8% of the population are Hindus, 19% are Muslims, 2.8% are Christians, and the remainder belong to other religions. The population exceeded 100,000 in the census of 1931 and grew by 20.5 per cent in the decade 1991–2001. As of 2011, the literacy rate of the city is 86.84 per cent, which is higher than the state's average of 75.6 per cent. Kannada is the most widely spoken language in the city. Approximately 19% of the population lives below the poverty line, and 9% live in slums. According to the 2001 census, 35.75% of the population in the urban areas of Karnataka are workers, but only 33.3% of the population of Mysore are. Members of Scheduled

Castes and Scheduled tribes constitute 15.1% of the population. According to the National Crime Records Bureau of India, the number of cognizable crime incidents reported in Mysore during 2010 was 3,407 (second in the state, after Bangalore's 32,188), increasing from 3,183 incidents reported in 2009.

Demography and Health

Between 1961 and 2001, the population of the district has been growing steadily and it has more than doubled from 1.14 million in 1961 to 2.64 million in 2001. In 2006, the district population has reached 2.87 million. Mysore taluk, because of the city of Mysore dominating it has had a population of 368,005 in 1961 which almost trebled to 1.04 million in 2001. The other taluks have witnessed similar tendencies to grow but some grew slower than others. For example, the population of H.D. Kote taluk has more than doubled in the 40 years since 1961, from 98,463 to 245,930. In 2006, this population has reached 265,992. With Mysore taluk accounting for nearly 40 per cent of the population of the district, the other taluks together have 60 per cent of the population of the district.

Looking at the decadal growth of the population in the district, there has been a drastic change in growth rates, from 28.4 per cent during 1961-71 to 24.48 per cent during 1981-91 and to 15.75 per cent during 1991-2001. In the middle of the decade 2001-11, the growth rate has come down to 8.29 per cent. Mysore taluk is the only taluk that registered a rate of growth of 10.41 per cent in the middle of the decade 2001-11, population primarily due to immigration. All other taluks have very quickly declined in growth rates which ranges from 19.18 per cent (T. Narasipura) to 47.33 per cent (H.D. Kote) during 1961-71 to 8.09 per cent (T. Narasipura) to 21.53 per cent (Mysore) during 1991-2001. In 2006, the growth rates have declined to 5.21 per cent in Hunsur taluk.

Improved performance of the district in regard to human health has been appreciable in that the life expectancy has increased from 62.9 years in 1991 to 69.30 years in 2006. During the period 1991-2001, the crude birth-rate declined from 26.9 births per thousand to 19.8 births per thousand. The drop in the crude death-rate during the same period has been from 8.3 deaths per thousand to merely 7.7 deaths per thousand. The infant mortality rate has declined to 56 per thousand from 79 infant deaths during 1991-2001.

The past few decades have witnessed a vast expansion of health / medical care infrastructure in the district. In 2005-06, there were 23 hospitals with 2,712 beds and 623 primary health care centers, serving the rural backwaters. Yet, the health / medical care infrastructure continues to be inadequate in both the rural and urban areas. Referral services are operative throughout the district. The health index for the district stood at 0.632 in 1991 and this has marginally risen to 0.663 in 2001. The district has in fact fallen behind the State in its health index in 2001 which the State has had an index of 0.680. In 2006, the health index of the district stood at 0.737, with Mysore taluk topping with 0.775 and Periyapatna taluk representing the bottom at 0.704. Nanjangud taluk being the one adjacent to Mysore taluk, especially the city, has shown 0.732 as its health index.

The district has registered a life expectancy at birth of 62.9 years (male 61.8 years, female 63.9 years - females are always better off in LEB than males) in 1991-92 and 64.8 years (male 62.8 years, female 66.3 years) in 2001-02.

In 2005-06, the district had a LEB of 69.3 years with Mysore taluk reporting 71.49 years, followed closely by Nanjangud taluk at 68.94 years, Hunsur taluk at 68.75 years, H.D. Kote taluk at 67.67 years and the least being reported for K.R. Nagar taluk 67.03 years.

The major diseases prevalent in district are malaria, typhoid, diarrhea, TB, leprosy, HIV and goiter. Reported cases of diseases in 2005-06 are: malaria 207, diarrhea 76,820, typhoid 994, TB 3,676, cholera 45, leprosy 178 and HIV 1,278.

Of these diseases, HIV is becoming a major threat and has the potential to destroy human capital. With 262 doctors, and a doctor-population ratio of 1:10,080, doctor-hospital ratio of 1.28, doctor-beds ratio of 1:20 and nurse-population ratio of 1:18,749, the district is especially facing growing health problem with newer diseases becoming endemic / epidemic.

Babies born underweight are an important indication of maternal malnutrition (or health problems such as gestation diabetes). The district .has recorded 806 babies born underweight in 2003-04, 736 in 2004-05 and 666 in 2005-06. The decline may be attributed to improving health / medical facilities, increasing awareness among pregnant women about nutrition and the government supply of nutritious food to pregnant women.

Table 4.2: Taluk-wise Decadal Growth of Population in Mysore District

Taluk	Year				
	1961-71	1971-81	1981-91	1991-2001	2001-06
Mysore	34.18	30.64	32.45	21.53	10.41
H.D. Kote	47.33	19.30	25.03	13.65	8.03
Hunsur	35.17	31.00	23.87	14.29	5.21
K. R. Nagar	19.86	15.72	18.25	10.04	6.84
Nanjangud	20.58	18.62	19.67	11.11	7.39
Periyapatna	21.50	34.42	21.80	18.71	6.78
T. Narasipura	19.18	20.84	17.14	8.09	7.13
District	28.40	25.12	24.48	15.75	8.29

Mysore district life expectancy at birth – 2006 Table 4.3:

Life Expectancy at Birth (LEB) in Mysore District

1991-92			2001-02		
Person	Male	Female	Person	Male	Female
62.9	61.8	63.9	64.8	62.8	66.3

Now-a-days mother and child care is a priority health programme not only for the district/State Governments but also for the urban and rural households. Total immunization of children is achieved in the country and the district has registered more than 100 per cent child immunization levels (102.6 per cent each in DPT and Polio, 106.1 per cent in BCG and 101.7 per cent in measles, for example) in the year 2005-06.

Table 4.4: Taluk-wise Health and Life Expectancy at Birth (LEB) 2005-06

Taluk	Health Index	Rank	LEB in Years	Rank
Mysore	0.775	1	71.49	1
H.D. Kote	0.711	4	67.67	4
Hunsur	0.729	3	68.75	3
K.R. Nagar	0.701	7	67.03	7
Nanjangud	0.732	2	68.94	2
Periyapatna	0.704	6	67.22	6
T. Narasipura	0.708	5	67.49	5
District (2006)	**0.737**	-	**69.30**	-

Source: Computed by using the health data provided by District Health Office, Mysore.

Economy

Tourism is the major industry in Mysore. The city attracted about 3.15 million tourists in 2010. Mysore has traditionally been home to industries such as weaving, sandalwood carving, bronze work and the production of lime and salt. The planned industrial growth of the city and the state was first envisaged at the *Mysore economic conference* in 1911. This led to the establishment of industries such as the Mysore Sandalwood Oil Factory in 1917 and the Sri Krishnarajendra Mills in 1920.

In a survey conducted in 2001 by *Business Today*, Mysore was ranked the fifth-best city in India in which to conduct business. For the industrial development of the city, the Karnataka Industrial Areas Development Board (KIADB) has established four industrial areas in and around Mysore, in the Belagola, Belawadi, Hebbal (Electronic City) and Hootagalli areas. Major industrial companies in Mysore include Infosys, Bharat Earth Movers, J.K.

Tyres, Wipro, Falcon Tyres, Larsen & Toubro, and Theorem India. There were setbacks when motorcycle manufacturer Ideal Jawa and the Sri Krishnarajendra Mills closed. Efforts have been made to revive them, such as the takeover of the Krishnarajendra Mills by the Atlantic Spinning and Weaving Mills, but they have run into other problems.

The growth of the information technology industry in the first decade of the 21st century has resulted in the city emerging as the second largest software exporter in Karnataka, next to Bangalore. The city contributed Rs. 1363 crore (US$275 million) to Karnataka's IT exports in the financial year 2009–2010. Infosys has established one of its major technical training centres in Mysore, and Wipro has established its Global Service Management Center (GSMC) there. Non-IT related services have been outsourced from other countries to companies in Mysore.

Income, Employment and Poverty

The per capita GDP of Mysore district at constant prices was Rs. 18,284 in 1999-2000 and it increased to Rs. 23,120 in 2005-06. The rank of the district of Mysore has improved from the 11th place to the 7th place in the State during this period. The percentage of population living below poverty line stood at 33 per cent in 2005-06 (as per ZP data).

Table gives a comparative picture of the growth rates of the economies of Karnataka State, Mysore district and taluks thereof. The table makes it clear that Hunsur taluk's TOP has grown at the highest rate (8.12 per cent) followed by Mysore taluk with 5.88 per cent growth rate. K.R. Nagar taluk witnessed the lowest growth rate of TOP (1.83 per cent), the next lowest growth rate of growth (4.33 per cent) recorded by T. Narasipura taluk.

The trends in the per capita of Karnataka State, Mysore district and of the taluks of Mysore district are presented in table. The per capita income of the Mysore district grew from Rs. 18,284 to Rs. 23,120 between 1999-2000 and 2005-06 at the compound growth rate of 3.99 per cent. The corresponding per capita incomes of the State for 1999-2000 and 2005-06 were Rs. 18,604 and Rs. 24,211, respectively. Thus Mysore district's per capita income continues to be lower than the State's per capita income.

The ACGR of Mysore district's per capita income (3.99 per cent) during the period 1999-2000 to2005-06 was lower than that of the state's per capita income (4.49 per cent). This clearly means that Mysore district's economy has grown at a slower rate than the State's economy. Talukwise trends are quite interesting. Hunsur taluk tops in economic growth, its per capita income, second only to Mysore taluk in absolute figures, has grown at the highest rate, 6.7 per cent per annum while that of Mysore taluk (while includes Mysore city) has grown at the rate of 4.5 per cent. The growth rate of the per capita income of K. R. Nagar taluk was the least, 0.49 per cent.

Table 4.5: Taluk-wise Economic Growth Rates in Mysore District

(Rs. in Lakhs)

Taluk	TDP in 1999-2000	TDP in 2005-06	ACGR (%)
H.D. Kote	33,831	45,824	5.19
Hunsur	42,019	67,130	8.12
K.R. Nagar	41,193	45,922	1.83
Mysore	212,178	299,107	5.88
Nanjangud	69,398	91,394	4.69
Periyapatna	34,333	46,355	5.13
T. Narasipura	39,661	51,161	4.33
Mysore District	**472,612**	**646,895**	**5.37**
Karnataka State	**9,622,900**	**13,556,300**	**5.87**

Table 4.6: Growth of Per capita income in Mysore District and Karnataka State at 1999-2000 prices

(Rs. in Lakhs)

Taluk	PCI 1999-2000 (Rs.)	PCI 2005-06 (Rs.)	ACGR (%)
H.D. Kote	14,055	17,591	3.81
Hunsur	16,909	24,955	6.70
K.R. Nagar	17,596	18,122	0.49
Mysore	20,877	27,184	4.50
Nanjangud	19,682	23,950	3.33
Periyapatna	15,641	19,150	3.43
T. Narasipura	14,523	17,308	2.97
Mysore District	**18,284**	**23,120**	**3.99**
Karnataka State	**18,604**	**24,211**	**4.49**

But the district's share in the State income is stagnant at almost 6 per cent through the 30 years. The shares of different sectors in the district income which stood at 35 per cent for the primary sector, 24.9 per cent for the secondary sector and 40.1 per cent for the tertiary sector in 1990-91, changed to 19.73 per cent, 29.64 per cent and 50.63 per cent, respectively, in 2005-06. For almost 25 years now, the primary sector has been shrinking, while the secondary sector has more or less stagnated and the tertiary sector has become the most important contributor to the district Income.

In 2001, the male workforce stood at 70.49 per cent and the female workforce stood at 29.51 per cent of the total workforce. The main male workers were at 83.42 per cent and marginal workers at 16.58 per cent of the total in 2001. Of the district population, the illiterates accounted for 36.52 per cent, non-workers accounted for 57.3 per cent, agricultural labourers for 27.03 per cent, marginal workers to total workers 16.58 per cent and the BPL families at 32.97 per cent, with a human poverty index (HPI) of 0.341. Among the taluks, the highest poverty index is represents for H.D. Kote taluk at 0.402, Nanjangud taluk at 0.426 and T. Narasipura at 0.450. The work participation rate stood at 42.02 per cent for the district with Hunsur representing 53.8 per cent (the highest among the taluks) and Mysore 35.58 per cent (the lowest among the taluks).The livelihood opportunity index for the district for the same year was 0.577, with Mysore taluk representing the highest index at 0.714 and T. Narasipura taluk the lowest index at 0.483.

The Livelihood Opportunity Index is computed by using the work participation ratio, percentage of main workers to total workers and percentage of other workers among main workers. This measure indicates the opportunities created in the taluk for work and reflects the standard of living enjoyed by the people in the taluk.

Greater employment opportunities are evident in the taluks which show higher Work Participation Rates (WPR). The higher WPR is found Hunsur (53.8 per cent) taluk followed by H.D. Kote (50.99 per cent), K.R. Nagar (46.96 per cent) and Periyapatna (45.51 per cent). The WPR in these taluks is higher than the State average. Lowest WPR is found in Mysore taluk (35.55 per cent) followed by T. Narasipura (38.7 per cent) and Nanjangud (43.37 per cent). The increasing trend in the WPR may be due to diversion from agricultural activities to more of non-agricultural activities. It is important to note that the Livelihood Opportunity Index for the taluks of the district is more than the State level LOI (0.438).

Education

Before the advent of the European system of education in Mysore, *agraharas* (Brahmin quarters) provided Vedic education to Hindus, and *madrassas* provided schooling for Muslims. Modern education began in Mysore when a free English school was established in 1833. In 1854 the East India Company promulgated the *Halifax Dispatch*, which suggested organising education based on the western model in the princely state of Mysore. The first college to be set up for higher education was the Maharajas College, founded in 1864. In 1868 the Mysore state decided to establish *hobli schools* to extend education to the masses. Under this scheme, a school providing free education was established in each *hobli* (a locality within the city). This led to the establishment of a *normal school* in Mysore which trained teachers to teach in the *hobli schools*.

A high school exclusively for girls was established in 1881 and later converted into the *Maharanis Women's College*. The *Industrial School*, the first institute for technical education in the city, was established in 1892; this was followed by the Chamarajendra Technical Institute in 1913. While the modern system of education was making inroads, colleges such as the *Mysore Sanskrit College*, established in 1876, continued to provide Vedic education.

The education system was enhanced by the establishment of the University of Mysore in 1916. This was the sixth university to be established in India and the first in Karnataka. It was named *Manasagangotri* ("fountainhead of the Ganges of the mind") by the poet Kuvempu. The university caters to the districts of Mysore, Mandya, Hassan and Chamarajanagar in Karnataka. About 127 colleges, with a total of 53,000 students, are affiliated with the university. Its alumni include Kuvempu, Gopalakrishna Adiga, S.L. Bhyrappa, U.R. Ananthamurthy and N.R. Narayana Murthy. Engineering education began in Mysore with the establishment in 1946 of the National Institute of Engineering, the second oldest engineering college in the state. The Mysore Medical College, founded in 1924, was the first medical college to be started in Karnataka and the seventh in India. Institutes of national importance in the city include the Central Food Technological Research Institute, the Central Institute of Indian Languages, the Defence Food Research Laboratory, and the All India Institute of Speech and Hearing.

Literacy and Education

Modern education started in 1833 with the establishment of a Free English School by the Palace of Mysore. The Kindergarten became popular as early as 1900. There is great emphasis on primary education, especially lower primary.

Trying to fulfill a Millennium Development Goal, Universal Primary Education is implemented through Sarva Shiksha Abhiyan (SSA). The girl-child gets priority in primary education.

Literacy rate for male was at 70.9 per cent in the district in 2001. This was a great improvement over the previous decades: from 39.3 per cent in 1981 and 59.71 per cent in 1991. The female literacy-rate was 55.81 per cent in the district in 2001. Showing greater strides, from 23 per cent in 1981 to 41.60 per cent in 1991. Mysore taluk tops the taluks while Nanjangud and H.D. Kote taluks are lagging behind. There is thus a gender inequality in literacy: male are more literate than female. There are variations in literacy in the rural and urban contexts, with urban areas in a more advantageous position: 82.80 per cent of urban against 51.84 per cent rural in 2001. Rural male literacy-rate was higher than rural female literacy-rate: 61.01 per cent against 42.31 per cent. The literacy gap between rural and urban areas at the district level is 30 per cent against 21.25 per cent at the State level in 2001.

Table 4.7 shows the gaps for three census years (1981, 1991 and 2001). In all the three years, the urban literacy rates have been far higher than the rural literacy rates, which are what they are expected to be, though for the district of Mysore the urban literacy rate was 56.93 per cent against 22 per cent for rural areas in 1981; 73.5 per cent urban against 36 per cent rural in 1991; and 82.80 per cent urban against 51.80 per cent rural in 2001.

Table 4.7: Taluk-wise Male and Female Literacy Rates for Mysore District 1981-2001

(in percentage)

Taluk	Male			Female		
	1981	1991	2001	1981	1991	2001
Mysore	56.9	73.47	81.58	43.6	60.07	71.02
H.D. Kote	27.7	46.97	61.95	12.0	26.41	43.44
Hunsur	37.5	54.77	67.53	717.4	31.93	48.06
K.R. Nagar	43.6	61.61	70.32	21.6	36.37	48.92
Nanjangud	32.0	45.77	57.24	15.7	27.52	41.70
Periyapatna	39.9	55.83	69.66	19.0	31.50	47.94
T. Narasipura	31.5	46.53	60.47	17.0	30.37	46.38
District	**39.3**	**59.71**	**70.9**	**23.0**	**41.60**	**55.81**

Source: Mysore District at a Glance, 1981, 1991 and 2001 (Census Data)

Table 4.8: Rural-Urban Literacy Gap (1981, 1991 and 2001)

Particulars	1981		1991		2001		Literacy Gap		
	Urban	Rural	Urban	Rural	Urban	Rural	1981	1991	2001
Mysore District	56.93	22.0	73.50	36.00	82.80	51.80	34.93	37.50	31.00
Karnataka State	-	-	74.20	47.69	80.58	59.30	-	26.51	21.25

Source: GOI, Census of India, 1981, 1991 and 2001

For the State, as a whole, the urban literacy rate was 74.2 per cent as against 47.69 per cent for rural in 1991 and 80.58 per cent for urban as against 59.3 per cent for rural in 2001. The increase in literacy rates in both urban and rural areas over the years in the district as well as State has been steady and appreciable. The extent of the gaps in literacy rates between the urban and the rural areas for the district as well as the State is as follows: for the district, the gap stood at 34.93 per cent in 1981 and went up to 37.5 per cent in 1991 only to decline to 31 per cent in 2001. For the State, the gap stood at 26.51 per cent in 1991 and declined to 21.25 per cent in 2001. Yet again the gaps in the district urban and rural literacy rates are far higher than in the State urban and rural literacy rates.

There are 2,386 primary schools, of which 79.21 per cent are run by the Department of Education, 5.03 per cent by private aided and 14.21 per cent by private unaided. In rural areas however there are 1,930 schools of which 88.86 per cent are government run. In all taluks, the primary schools are accessible from all habitations and are available to all sections of the population. In regard to high schools, however, the access rates are below 100 per cent, 95.38 per cent for the district and at cent per cent for Mysore taluk. There are high schools which are not accessible to some. High school education is however affordable throughout the district. Gross enrollment ratio is at 108.01 per cent for boys and 105.48 per cent for girls. The retention rate for all in the district is 97.81 per cent, with 97.97 per cent for boys and 97.63 per cent for girls at the lower primary schools. Dropout rates at the lower primary schools are 2.19 per cent for all, 2.37 per cent for girls and 2.03 per cent for boys. Throughout the taluks, the reported dropout rates are small, not more than 6 per cent.

There are 452 secondary schools. Only 32.97 per cent of them are run by the Government while 21.46 per cent are aided private and 44.03 per cent are unaided private. While 39 per cent of the teachers are males, the rest of them are females. Pupil-teacher ratio in the district is 29:1, which is around the same in all the taluks. All teachers in position are trained. To a certain extent, the education at the primary and secondary levels is free and also especially in the government schools. On the other hand, education at the aided private schools are relatively cheap than in unaided private schools. Free textbooks and free uniforms are provided to a small number of students. There have been several programmes for improving the quality of education in the schools. Girl child gets preferential treatment in education as well, thanks to the recent gender-sensitization.

Mysore district registered the highest literacy rate of 63.48 per cent, which is second only to the state average of 66.64 per cent in 2001. Within the district, the patterns of temporal change in the literacy rates are identical: that is, Mysore taluk tops the taluks of the district with the highest literacy-rate are in all the three censuses. K.R. Nagar taluk comes closest with the next highest rates for the three census years, while H.D. Kote taluk had the lowest total literacy rate of 20 per cent in 1981, Nanjangud taluk had the lowest rates in the censuses 1991 (36.83 per cent) and 2001 (49.95 per cent). Overall, the performance of Periyapatna taluk is commendable in that its literacy rates have doubled (from as low as 30 per cent to almost to 60 per cent) in the 20 years between 1981 and 2001. Hunsur taluk does not lag far behind either.

Urban areas of Mysore taluk followed by K. R. Nagar show a high rate of literacy in 2001 with 84.38 per cent and 81.41 per cent, respectively. T. Narasipura taluk (67.98 per cent) and Periyapatna taluk (74.44 per cent) recorded relatively low urban literacy rates compared to other. The literacy rate among the male (87.33 per cent) and female (78.12 per cent) in urban Mysore district is above the state average of 74.13 per cent in 2001. The literacy rate of male and female (88.55 per cent and 80.08 per cent, respectively) is the highest in urban Mysore taluk in 2001.

The literacy rate for the rural Mysore district is much lower than that of its urban counterpart. It is almost half that for the urban literacy rate in 2001, at 42.31 per cent for female population and three-fourths of the urban literacy rate in 2001, at 61.01 per cent, for male population. Because of the relatively high concentration of educational institutions in the urban areas vis-à-vis to the rural areas in the district, the urban literacy rates is more than the rural literacy rates.

Table 4.9: Educational Institutions in Mysore District in 2006

(in Numbers)

Educational Institutions	Numbers
Primary Schools	2386
High Schools	471
Pre-University Colleges	108
Polytechniques	9
General Colleges (science & arts)	22
Physical Educational Colleges	2
Engineering Colleges	4
Medical Colleges	2
Dental Colleges	2
Colleges of Indian Medicines	2
Central Education Institution	2
D Ed institution	32
B Ed colleges	15
DIET	1
Research Centre	4
University	2

Source: Mysore District at a Glance

Table 4.10: Taluk-wise Educational Indicators 2006

Taluk	Literacy rate (%)			Enrollment rate (%)			Education Index	EDEI (GDI)
	Male	Female	Person	Male	Female	Person		
Mysore	84.60	77.82	81.26	80.46	82.57	81.50	0.814	0.813
H.D. Kote	70.34	55.57	63.05	70.61	64.80	67.65	0.646	0.641
Hunsur	74.30	59.82	67.16	70.26	68.86	69.57	0.680	0.675
K.R. Nagar	73.53	56.37	64.91	73.34	74.49	73.90	0.679	0.674
Nanjangud	63.40	50.87	57.19	70.81	72.04	71.41	0.619	0.617
Periyapatna	76.37	60.30	68.68	63.87	63.81	63.84	0.671	0.667
T. Narasipura	68.13	56.75	62.50	68.25	71.73	69.93	0.650	0.649
District	**75.43**	**65.67**	**69.68**	**73.75**	**74.45**	**74.26**	**0.713**	**0,716**

Note: Literacy rate is computed for 7+ population and enrollment rate is for
primary, secondary and tertiary (PUE) only. EDEI is equally distributed
education index (GDI)

A comparative analysis of rural and urban literacy rates indicates that the rural areas are in a disadvantageous position because of lack or inadequacy of the educational infrastructure and poor socio-economic status of rural people while urban areas are favourably placed. Nevertheless, the phenomenon of literate and the educated gravitating towards towns and cities must also be borne in mind while explaining the higher levels of urban literacy vis-à-vis rural literacy. Concentration of the literates and also the educational infrastructure make way for higher levels of literacy in urban areas.

According to the index computed, the district education index is 0.713 whereas the equally distributed education index (EDEI or GDI) is 0.716, which place the district higher up the ladder of human development in comparison with other districts of Karnataka State. While Mysore taluk has an education index (0.814) larger than that of the district, all other taluks have smaller indices that of the district index. When considered, the district does slightly better in terms of EDEI or GDI at 0.716 but all the taluks, including Mysore taluk, than in terms of EI perform less better with values less than the corresponding ELS. This once again reiterates the relative positions of men and women and boys and girls (gender) with girls and women doing less better in education than boys and girls. This calls for a concerted effort at improving female education in the district.

Housing, Water Supply and Sanitation

In 2001, the number of census houses in the district was 709,225 of which 443,922 were in rural areas and 265,303 were in urban areas. As many as 79.71 per cent of the, households lived in own houses whereas 17.39 per cent of them were in rented housing. Apart 92.65 per cent of the households had own houses in T. Narasipura taluk, while only 61.85 per cent of the households in Mysore taluk had own houses. The city of Mysore has a very large number of households living in rented housing (33.18 per cent). The tenure status of households in urban areas of Mysore district in 2001 was of the order of 55.5 per cent for own housing and 39.08 per cent for rented housing. T. Narasipura taluk has the largest proportion of the urban households living in their own housing (71.95 per cent) while Mysore taluk has the least (53.38 per cent). The two taluks reversed the order in respect of rented housing with 40.53 per cent in Mysore taluk and 23.7 per cent in T. Narasipura taluk. The tenure status of the rural households has shown better ownership housing (99.50 per cent) than rented housing (8.45 per cent) in the year 2001. All the taluks except K.R. Nagar taluk have shown better prospects with more than 90 per cent of ownership housing while the Mysore taluk has shown the highest proportion of rented housing (26.71 per cent) for the rural households.

Census 2001 has recorded proportions of households residing in different types of housing, namely, permanent (56.75 per cent), semi-permanent (37.8 per cent) and temporary (5.44 per cent). Hunsur taluk has shown the largest of 75.55 per cent of the households living in permanent housing, K.R. Nagar taluk has the largest share of the semi-permanent housing at 63.35 per cent, Nanjangud taluk has largest of temporary housing at 11.82 per cent of the households living in. In urban areas of district, permanent housing has been accounted for by 82.22 per cent of households, semi-permanent housing by 15.41 per cent of households and temporary housing by 2.36 per cent of the households in the district.

Mysore taluk has the largest of urban households living in permanent housing (85.79 per cent), Hunsur taluk has the largest of urban households living in semi-permanent housing (39.37 per cent) and T. Narasipura taluk has the largest of urban households living in temporary housing (7.29 per cent). Rural areas of the district have their own typical distribution of permanent housing (38.33 per cent), semi-permanent housing (55.03 per cent) and temporary housing (6.63 per cent) and the taluks do show variations as in the earlier cases, total district and urban areas of the district.

It is important to mention that the socioeconomic inequalities among the different communities of the district and imbalances amidst the marginalized social groups are reflected in the types of housing they are living in. Scheduled castes of Mysore for example show remarkable variations in types of housing as well as across the taluks: permanent housing 16.97 per cent, semi-permanent housing 47.76 per cent and temporary 35.27 per cent. Housing is a measure of inequality in the access to rights including: right to the shelter. Interesting, the scheduled tribes also show a similar, more or less unequal pattern of distribution of housing. Inequalities and imbalances are also manifest in the materials used for housing.

The gap between the demand for and supply of housing has been widening fast with increasing population and with the purchasing power of the people. In recent years, there has been a real-estate boom that the middle class has been buying up lands and residential properties at high prices and have been developing housing primarily as a response to finances being made available from banks at affordable interest rates. The State and Central Governments have introduced several schemes for the houseless and the site-less, such as the Ashraya, Matsya Ashraya and Ambedkar Schemes. The Ashraya and the Ambedkar Schemes are also operational in the urban areas of the district. One of the criticisms changed against the public housing schemes is that the constructions are substandard because they are contracted to unscrupulous. The criticism against private housing schemes is that they are expensive and unaffordable for the common people. The plight of the houseless is worrisome for they mostly belong to the marginalized social groups, who were and are being exploited by the vested interests.

In regard to total households in the district with and without toilet access, there are details by taluks. While 22.2 per cent of the district households (84,679) have access to sanitation, a large majority of 77.8 per cent do not have it (297) 50 households). Among the families with access to sanitation, Mysore taluk has the largest number (17,075 or 31.1 per cent) followed closely by T. Narasipura taluk (14,850 or 26.8 per cent) and Nanjangud taluk (12,403 or 26.8 per cent) in regard to taluk households. K.R. Nagar taluk has the least proportion of households with access at 16.3 per cent (or 11,948 households). The taluks with no access to toilets in the order of their neglect is as follows: K.R. Nagar (83.7 per cent), H.D. Kote (82.3 per cent), Periyapatna (79.7 per cent), Nanjangud (73.2 per cent), T. Narasipura (73.2 per cent), Hunsur (72 per cent) and Mysore (68.9 per cent).

The access to different sources of drinking water shows great variations across the sources and across the taluks. Access at the district level to tap water is therefore 59.5 per cent of the rural population; access to hand pump 25.8 per cent of the rural population is tube well 7.83 per cent; access to well 5.02 per cent and other sources 1.85 per cent of the population. On the other hand, access in regard to tap water is to 90.96 per cent, hand pump 4.79 per cent, tube well 2.86 per cent, well 0.33 per cent and other sources to 1.08 per cent of the urban population of the district. In the taluks, tap water and water from the hand pumps are a major source of water in the rural areas. There were 1,349 tube wells, 1,073 minor water supply projects and 9,862 hand pumps in use during 2005-06. Nearly 60 per cent of the villages (habitations) received more than 55 lpcd water and the rest habitations receive water little higher than 35 lpcd. That it is *very* important to note that in summer season about 30 per cent of the habitations receive less than 25 lpcd water. However the Zilla Panchayat has implemented several programmes to meet the requirements of safe drinking water in the district particularly in summer season. Water supplied in the urban areas of the district is only tap water.

Gender Issues and Human Development

Women and girls are traditionally respected and loved among the households. Yet their relative position continues as dependents, subordinates and not as equals, even among the progressive households and the communities. In fact, in economically well off homes, their position has been more precarious than in the poorer homes where, women as bread-winners along with men and boys, often get better treatment and respect. With increasing globalization women and even girls are asserting their rights and do get a semblance of respect. In recent years, however, women of the world, and country for that matter, have risen as one body against the inequality and they have also been successful to a certain extent. What is even more important is that men and boys are beginning to notice their relevance and steadfastness that women and girls today are better off. Mysore, being a society of moderates, is sitting up and is moving in the cause of women and girls. They are getting the respect and love they deserve and they are, for their part, doing everything that would make them 'equal' in all respects. They are indeed on the way to it.

Gender-related Development Index (GDI) has been a measure of human development, meaning that the relationship between gender and human development is strong. However, it is well-known that a high HDI ranking is not always matched by a high GDI ranking and that is true of Mysore district as well. Women and girls of the district are less than one half of the total population, they were 48.94 per cent of the total population in urban areas and 49.1 per cent in the rural areas according to census 2001. In no taluk of the district, does the female population exceeded 50 per cent. In urban Mysore district, the highest share of female population was in Nanjangud taluk at 49.43 per cent and the lowest share was in H.D. Kate taluk at 48.61 per cent. Mysore taluk accounted for only 49.11 per cent of the total population in 2001.

As for children of 0-6 years age group, girl-children accounted for 49.21 per cent of the total population of 0-6 years age in 1991, decreased to 49.02 per cent of the total 0-6 years population in 2001. That girl-children were on the marginal decrease over the decade 19912001. Sex-ratio of the has a gradually increased over the last 30 years, from 936 in 1971 to 952 in 1981, to 953 in 1991 and to 965 in 2001.

Table 4.11: Percentage of Female Population to Total Population in Mysore District 2001

Taluk	Percentage of female population to total population	
	Urban	Rural
Mysore	**49.11**	**48.99**
H.D. Kote	48.61	49.32
Hunsur	48.98	49.75
K.R. Nagar	49.06	49.69
Nanjangud	49.43	48.95
Periyapatna	49.06	48.25
T. Narasipura	49.38	48.86
District	**48.94**	**49.10**

Source: Mysore District at a Glance

Education of women and girls has also shown tremendous increase in that the literacy rate of 23 per cent in 1981 improved to 40.60 in 1991 and to 55.81 in 2001, an increase of 32.81 per cent over the 20 years. Urban female literacy has also shown a corresponding improvement from 49.98 per cent in 1981 to 66.91 per cent in 1991 and 78.12 per cent in 2001. All taluks of the district have shown the same vigour and intensity in their improvement in female education. H.D. Kote, T. Narasipura and Periyapatna taluks were the low performers when compared to other taluks. Literacy rates in rural areas showed improvements over the years but at much lower levels: 12.92 per cent in 1981 to 25.53 per cent in 1991 and 42.31 per cent in 2001. Spatial variations in rural female literacy rates are as high as in urban areas, although at slightly lower level. Parents are increasingly recognizing the need to educate girl-children and are coming out of their traditional stereotype culture to a much matured and sophisticated culture. They can be said to be fully aware of the responsibility of the parenthood and encourage girl-children to compete in the male-dominated society. And as it is quite evident, girls are much better competitors today than they were 20 years ago.

As for human health, women and girls are better equipped to withstand hardships so that their life expectancy at birth was 63.9 years against the male's at 61.8 years in 1991 and it rose to 66.3 years as against 62.8 years for males in 2001. The computed figures for 2005-06 show that the life expectancy at birth for female was 71.28 per cent against the males at 67.43.

Table 4.12: Life Expectancy at Birth (LEB) in Mysore

Life Expectancy at Birth (LEB) in Mysore (Years)								
1991			2001			2006*		
Person	Male	Female	Person	Male	Female	Person	Male	Female
62.9	61.8	63.9	64.8	62.8	66.3	69.30	67.43	71.28

Note: Computed for 2005-06
Source: KHDR 2005

Women work-participation rates were 22.73 per cent for main workers and 61.96 per cent for marginal workers in 2001. The variations shown by the taluks in the work-participation rates were between 13.64 per cent (T. Narasipura taluk) and 33.56 per cent (H.D. Kote taluk) while Mysore taluk registered a much lower rate at 22.66 per cent for the main workers. As for the marginal workers, the lowest participation rate was in T Narasipura (43.02 per cent) and the highest was in Periyapatna at 76.66 per cent in the year 2001. Women formed 27.86 per cent of the cultivators, 49.31 per cent of the agricultural labourers and 38.41 per cent workers of the household industries. Women in other works accounted for 24.39 per cent in 2001.

Women and girls are deprived of both livelihoods and health to a great extent. Access to toilets was restricted to 44.13 per cent, with access limited to 18.89 per cent of women in H.D. Kote taluk and 77.76 per cent of them in Mysore taluk.

The one area where women have begun to exercise their rights is at the local governance. There are increasingly larger number of women contesting local elections on party basis but unfortunately where they have to exercise their powers in governance, they give way to their husbands and/or sons, frittering away the opportunity to govern and do good. In 2005-06 there were 43 of them in position as municipal representatives, with 10 of them in Nanjangud taluk and 9 of them in K.R. Nagar taluk. The representatives are from various communities, especially socially marginalized communities.

As for the gender in Gram Panchayats from the marginalized groups, the SC men members (484) account for 12.28 per cent of the Gram Panchayat membership and SC women for 9.68 per cent. ST women out-number (323 members, 8.2 per cent) ST men (309 members, 7.84 per cent). Overall, the marginalized groups of SCs and STs together have about 40 per cent of the total Gram Panchayat membership. As to their effective leadership and functioning, do the Gram Panchayat members from the marginalized social groups act independently or allow themselves to be influenced by the upper class members in office? The upper castes do exercise an influence lasting in impact and value

Among the total Gram Panchayat members in office in 2005-06, men dominated with 57.35 per cent as against women members at 42.65 per cent in the district. However, the present of representation of women satisfies the 30 per cent representation for women at the grassroots level of governance. But the serious question is: do women really exercise their power and act in responsibility or just give their power away to men? Looking at the numbers of men and women, the taluk-wise distribution appears to be a fair deal for women; Mysore taluk has

395 men and 297 women in office. The next largest number for men and also women is in T. Narasipura taluk with 353 men against 277 women. The least number of grass roots members is found in Periyapatna taluk with 291 men and 210 women representatives in the Gram Panchayats.

Mysore city has achieved considerable progress in attaining the Millennium development goals. Some of the Key Health indicators pertaining to state are shown in the following table.

Table 4.13: Health indicators of City in 2012-13

Sl.No.	Name of Disease/Cause of morbidity (e.g. COPD, trauma, cardiovascular disease etc.)	Number of cases admitted in 2012
1.	Injuries and Trauma	NA
2.	Self inflicted injuries/suicide	NA
3.	Cardiovascular Disease	04
4.	Cancer (Breast cancer)	NA
5.	Cancer (cervical cancer)	04
6.	Cancer (other types)	NA
7.	Mental health and depression	NA
8.	Chronic Obstructive Pulmonary Disease (COPD)	NA
9.	Malaria	24
10.	Dengue	2
11.	Infectious fever (like H1N1, avian influenza, etc.)	5
12.	TB	3347
13.	MDR TB	0
14.	Diarrhea and gastroenteritis	370
15.	Jaundice/Hepatitis	0
16.	Skin diseases	33
17.	Severely Acute Malnourishment (SAM)	0
18.	Iron deficiency disorder	14
19.	Others	92(IDSP)

Source: IDSP reports

Mysore City Corporation has taken key decision to cover the City areas based on the Health Vulnerability, Migration of population, and adverse events on health of the people for communicable and non-communicable disease prevalence, existence of underserved population in the cities. City PHC areas with Population and availability of Basic services for 2013-14 NUHM planning are shown in the following table.

Table 4.14: City PHC area

Sl. No	Ward No	Name of the Slum CHC/PHC	Population	Quality of Housing (Kutcha/Pucca/Mixed)	Quality of Sanitation (IHL,Community Toilets, OD)	Status of Water Supply (Piped, Hand Pumps, Open Wells, None)	Location & Distance of nearest AWC	Location & Distance of Nearest Promary School	Location & Distance of Nearest PHC/UHP/UFWC
1	15	MMK	24517	Mixed	Community Tiolets	Piped	with in area	3 km HPS	PHC 6 km
	16			Mixed	Community Tiolets	Piped	7 km	1 km hps	PHC 8 km
	17			Mixed	Community Tiolets	Piped	4 km	1 km	PHC 5 km
	18			Mixed	Community Tiolets	Piped	2 km	½ km	PHC 3 km
	19			Mixed	Community Tiolets	Piped	1 km	2 km	PHC 2 km
2	34	AIWC	22800	Mixed	Community Tiolets	Piped	With in the area AWC Center No 4	With in the area hps	PHC 2 km
	39			Mixed	Community Tiolets	Piped	With in the area AWC Center No 4	With in the area hps	PHC 2 km
3	29	PHC Bannimantapa	12456	Mixed	Community Tiolets	Piped	With in the area AWC Center No 2	1 km hPS	PHC 3 ½ km
	44			Mixed	Community Tiolets	Piped	3 km in AWC no 3	With in the area hps	PHC 1 km
	45			Mixed	Community Tiolets	Piped	With in the area AWC Center No 5	2 km hps	PHC 3 km
4	46	Rajendranagara	10549	Mixed	Community Tiolets	Piped	With in the area AWC Center No 5	With in the area	PHC 2 km
	47			Mixed	Community Tiolets	Piped	With in the area AWC Center No 3	With in the area	With in the area
5	59	Shanthinagara	10480	Mixed	Community Tiolets	Piped	1 km in AWC Center No 2	2 km hps	PHC 2 km
	44			Mixed	Community Tiolets	Piped	With in the area AWC Center No 2	1 km hps	PHC 2 km
6	7	Krishnamurty Puram	9814	Mixed	Community Tiolets	Piped	With in the area AWC Center No 5	With in the area	With in the area
	8			Mixed	Community Tiolets	Piped	With in the area	With in the area	With in the area
7	51	Laskar 'B' Gandhinagara	3669	Mixed	Community Tiolets	Piped	With in the area AWC Center No 6	With in the area	With in the area
	50	Laskar 'B' Gandhinagara	3669	Mixed	Community Tiolets	Piped	With in the area AWC Center No 5	With in the area	With in the area

Table 4.14 (continued)

Sl. No	Ward No	Name of the Slum CHC/PHC	Population	Quality of Housing (Kutcha/Pucca/Mixed)	Quality of Sanitation (IHL,Community Toilets, OD)	Status of Water Supply (Piped, Hand Pumps, Open Wells, None)	Location & Distance of nearest AWC	Location & Distance of Nearest Promary School	Location & Distance of Nearest PHC/UHP/UFWC
8	30	Laskar 'A' Gandhinagara							
		Manjunathapuram	3500	Mixed	Community Tiolets	Piped	With in the area	With in the area	PHC 3 km
	31	Gokulam 3 rd stage Swiper Colony	638	Mixed	Community Tiolets	Piped	With in the area	With in the area	PHC 3 km
	31	South of Kumbarakoppal	1400	Mixed	Community Tiolets	Piped	With in the area	1 k m hps	PHC 3 ½ km
	35	Devarajmohalla	400	Mixed	Community Tiolets	Piped	1 km AWC	2 k m hps	PHC 2 ½ km
9	27	PHC Kumbarakoppa	36232						
	27	Byraveswaranagara		Mixed	Community Tiolets	Piped	2 k m AWC	1 km hpc	PHC 2 k m
	27	Lokanatha nagara		Mixed	Community Tiolets	Piped	With in the area	1 km hps	PHC 2 km
	27	Hebbal colony		Mixed	Community Tiolets	Piped	With in the area	1 km hps	PHC 2 km
	26	Lakshmikanthnagara		Mixed	Community Tiolets	Piped	With in the area	5 km hps	PHC 6 km
	28			Mixed	Community Tiolets	Piped	With in the area AWC Center No 4	1 km hps	PHC 1 km
10	3	K R Center	3907	Mixed	Community Tiolets	Piped	4 km AWC	3 km hps	PHC 4 km

Source: Health and Family Welfare Services, Mysore District. Implementation Plan for 2013-2014. Mysore City.

Health infrastructure exists in the form of Government health facilities, Health facilities of City local bodies, Donor agencies and NGO's catering facilities. Still then large gap exist in coverage of the city population by the Government facilities some of the state allocations also come from City RCH component under NRHM-RCH Flexible Pool to serve the community information for the focused above mentioned city areas the overview of the Existing Infrastructures was indicated in the following table.

Table 4.15: Overview of the existing infrastructure in the city areas

Sl. No.	Name & type of facility	Managing Authority	Location of Health facility	Population covered by the facility	Services provided
1.	PHC-Kumbara Koppalu	Govt Health Department	Kumbara Koppalu	58102	OPD, Lab services, General Health
2.	Mahila Makkala Koota	Govt Health Department	Mahila Makkala Koota	64774	OPD, Lab services, General Health
3	A I W C	MUDA	A I W C	43912	OPD, Lab services, General Health
4	I.P.P 8-Bannimantap	Govt Health Department	Bannimantap	40272	OPD, Lab services, General Health
5	I.P.P 8 Rajendra Nagar	Govt Health Department	Rajendra Nagar	27382	OPD, Lab services, General Health
6	I.P.P 8-Shanthi Nagar	Govt Health Department	Shanthi Nagar	58452	OPD, Lab services, General Health
7	PHC-KrishnaMurthy Puram	MUDA	KrishnaMurthy Puram	19188	OPD, Lab services, General Health
8	K R Center	MUDA	K R Center	52747	OPD, Lab services, General Health
9	Corporation Lashkar - B	MUDA	Corporation Lashkar - B	48065	OPD, Lab services, General Health
10	Corporation Lashkar - A	MUDA	Corporation Lashkar - A	51102	OPD, Lab services, General Health

Source: Health and Family Welfare Services, Mysore District. Implementation Plan for 2013-2014. Mysore City.

State has also spend on Health care of the city through Infrastructure maintenance for City Family Welfare Centres (UFWCs) and Health dispensaries the details are shown in the following table.

Table 4.16: State's Allocation under Infrastructure Maintenance (Treasury Route) head

FMR Code	Activity	Amount Approved in 2012-13 (Rs in Lakhs)	Amount Approved in 2013-14 (Rs in Lakhs)
Infrastructure Maintenance		Nil	Nil
1.	City Family Welfare Centres (UFWCs)	4	4
2.	City Revamping Scheme (Health Posts)	Nil	Nil
	Total	4	4

Source: Health and Family Welfare Services, Mysore District. Implementation Plan for 2013-2014. Mysore City.

In spite of above measures there is still inequality exist for health care to city poor. Out of pocket expenditure is increasing to city poor for availing Health facilities which need to be addressed.

Key Public Health Priorities, Challenges and Actions adopted

Mysore city has undocumented high migratory population as land inside the city is costly for rent or occupation people tent to settle in peri city areas which come under the preview of Mysore city. City also faces staff deficiency to cater basic Health services even to mother and child. Large number of underserved areas having vulnerable population, sexuality minorities need to be mapped for providing focused Health services.

Table 4.17: Key public health priorities challenges and action adopted

Priorities	Challenges	Actions adopted
Infrastructure Strengthening and improve the services	Migratory population, Vulnerable Populations	Provision was made to cover the population under NUHM
Manpower Strengthening and recruitment	Economical constraints and lack of adequate manpower	Provisions are made for New PHCs
Providing health care services to Slums and Underserved Areas	Identifying the beneficiary	Mapping and Survey of local slums through independent agency

Source: Health and Family Welfare Services, Mysore District. Implementation
Plan for 2013-2014. Mysore City.

NUHM – Goals, Objectives, Strategies and Outcomes

Mysore City is focusing on City Health for this there are certain Goals, Objectives, Strategies and Out comes they are in lien with the National and Mysore goals.

Goals: City aim to improve the health status of the city population in general, but particularly of the poor and other disadvantaged sections. City will concentrate on facilitating equitable access and quality health care through a revamped public health system, partnerships with private, community based mechanism with the active involvement of the city local bodies.

Objectives: Mysore city has similar objectives like NRHM, JNNURM, and ICDS they are

1. To provide health care to poor and underserved in city area.

2. To reduce IMR and MMR in city area.

3. Improving Human resources and Infrastructure in City areas to improve Health care.

Strategies: Mysore has some strategies they are as follows

1. Improving the efficiency of public health system in the cities by strengthening, revamping and rationalizing existing government primary city health structure and designated referral facilities.

2. Promotion of access to improved health care at household level through community based groups; Mahila Arogya Samitis.

3. Strengthening public health through innovative preventive and promotive action.

4. Increased access to health care through creation of revolving fund.

5. IT enabled services (ITES) and e-governance for improving access improved surveillance and monitoring.

6. Capacity building of stakeholders.

7. Prioritizing the most vulnerable amongst the poor.

8. Ensuring quality health care services.

Outcomes: The Mysore would strive to put in place a sustainable city health delivery system under NUHM for addressing the health concerns of the city poor.

1. Attain the aimed achievement in establishment in Inputs for Institutional strengthening.

2. Strengthen the Capacity building through Quality training programmes from existing infrastructures.

3. Output level indicators are set to achieve optimal OPD care and reach city poor by Outreach camps.

4. Impact level will focus on city poor.

Plan for Poor in City area

Mysore City area has 9.83 lakh population. Among them 1.7 lakh are slum and under served population Most of these people are Lower middle class. But their Income status is not known. There are cluster of undeclared slums present which needs to be mapped for catering health services.

The following are the list of hospitals in Mysore which treat patients under Mediclaim of private insurance and some government schemes.

Table 4.18: List of private sector hospitals and nursing homes in Mysore

Sl.No.	Name of the Hospital/Nursing home
1	Aadithya Adhikari Hospital
2	Adarsh Hospital - Mysore
3	Akshaya Nursing Home - Mysore
4	Aravinda Hospital
5	Ashwini Nursing Home - Mysore
6	B G S Apollo Hospitals
7	Bahusar Nursing Home
8	Basappa Memorial Hospital
9	BGS Apollo Hospitals
10	Bhagwan Mahaveer Darshan Eye Hospital
11	Bharath Hospital and Institute of Oncology
12	Bibi Ayesha Milli Hospital
13	C S I Holdsworth Memorial Hospital
14	Cauvery Hospital [Fortis]
15	Chaitra Hospital - Mysore
16	Chandrakala Hospital and Institute of Medical Research
17	Chitra Hospital - Mysore
18	Chitras Hospital
19	City Bone and Joint Centre
20	Columbia Asia Hospital
21	Dr Lalitha Memorial Chamundeshwari Nursing Home
22	Dr Ramesh Hospital for Piles and Proctology
23	Gopal Gowda Shanthaveri Memorial Hospital
24	Gopal Nursing Home and Heart Centre
25	Harsha Hospital - Mysore
26	Hitech Kidney Stone Hospital - Mysore
27	Holy Cross Hospital - Kamagere
28	Indira Nursing Home - Mysore
29	J S S Hospital - Mysore
30	Kamakshi Hospital

Sl.No.	Name of the Hospital/Nursing home
31	Karuna Hospital - Mysore
32	Mahadeshwara Nursing Home
33	Minds Hospital
34	Murthy Eye Hospital
35	Mythri Hospital - Mysore
36	Nanjamma Javaregowda Hospital
37	Netra Jyothi Eye Hospital
38	Narayana Multi Speciality Hospital
39	New Adarsha Hospital
40	NJ Hospital
41	Pragathi Vision - Super Speciality Eye Hospital
42	Priyadarshani General Hospital
43	Ramakrishan Hospital
44	Raman Memorial Hospital
45	Relife Hospital
46	Riverview Healthcare Pvt Ltd - Mysore
47	Sita Ranga Nursing Home
48	Sri Annapoorna Nursing Home
49	Sri Chamundeshwari Maternity and Nursing Home
50	Srinivasa Maternity Home
51	St Joseph's Hospital
52	Surya Hospital - Mysore
53	Sushrutha Eye Hospital
54	Sushrutha Ortho Care
55	Thulasi Janardhan Memorial Hospital
56	Usha Kiran Eye Hospital and Usha Kiran Charitable Trust
57	Vaatsalya Hospital - Mysore
58	Vidisha Nursing Home - Mysore
59	Vidyaranya Hospital Pvt Ltd Mysore
60	Vijayanagara Nursing Home
61	Vikram Hospital and Heart Centre
62	Vikram Jeev Hospital for Gastrointestinal Disease
63	Vikram Orthopaedic Hospital Pvt Ltd
64	Vivekananda Memorial Hospital

Apart from the above, the state run hospitals such as Krishnaraja Hospital, Cheluvamba Hospital, PKTB Sanitorium and Jayadeva Institute for Cardio-Science are serving the health care needs of the citizens of Mysore. The railways have a separate hospital. There is an ESI Hospital to cater to those who are covered under the Employees State Insurance Act.

CHAPTER – V

THE EXISTING HEALTH SERVICES SYSTEM

5.1 INTRODUCTION

The health care system in India is characterised by multiple systems of medicine, mixed ownership patterns and different kinds of delivery structures. Public sector ownership is divided between central and state governments, municipal and *Panchayat* local governments. Public health facilities include teaching hospitals, secondary level hospitals, first-level referral hospitals (CHCs or rural hospitals), dispensaries; primary health centres (PHCs), sub-centres, and health posts. Also included are public facilities for selected occupational groups like organized work force (ESI), defence, government employees (CGHS), railways, post and telegraph and mines among others. The private sector (for profit and not for profit) is the dominant sector with 50 per cent of people seeking indoor care and around 60 to 70 per cent of those seeking ambulatory care (or outpatient care) from private health facilities. While India has made significant gains in terms of health indicators - demographic, infrastructural and epidemiological, it continues to grapple with newer challenges. Not only have communicable diseases persisted over time but some of them like malaria have also developed insecticide-resistant vectors while others like tuberculosis are becoming increasingly drug resistant. HIV/AIDS have of late assumed extremely virulent proportions. The 1990s have also seen an increase in mortality on account of non-communicable diseases arising as a result of lifestyle changes. The country is now in the midst of a dual disease burden of communicable and non-communicable diseases. This is coupled with spiralling health costs, high financial burden on the poor and erosion in their incomes. Around 24% of all people hospitalized in India in a single year fall below the poverty line due to hospitalization. An analysis of financing of hospitalization shows that large proportion of people; especially those in the bottom four income quintiles borrow money or sell assets to pay for hospitalization.[1]

This situation exists in a scenario where health care is financed through general tax revenue, community financing, out of pocket payment and social and private health insurance schemes. India spends about 4.9% of GDP on *Regional Overview in South-East Asia Page 80* health.[2] The per capita total expenditure on health in India is US$ 23, of which the per capita Government expenditure on health is US$ 4. Hence, it is seen that the total health expenditure is around 5% of GDP, with breakdown of public expenditure (0.9%); private expenditure (4.0%). The private expenditure can be further classified as out-of-pocket (OOP) expenditure (3.6%) and employees/community financing (0.4%). It is thus evident that public health investment has been comparatively low. In fact as a percentage of GDP it has declined from 1.3% in 1990 to 0.9% as at present. Furthermore, the central budgetary allocation for health (as a percentage of the total Central budget) has been stagnant at 1.3% while in the states it has declined from 7.0% to 5.5%.

In light of the fiscal crisis facing the government at both central and state levels, in the form of shrinking public health budgets, escalating health care costs coupled with demand for health-care services, and lack of easy access of people from the low-income group to quality health care, health insurance is emerging as an alternative mechanism for financing of health care.

5.2 HEALTH SYSTEM IN INDIA: OPPORTUNITIES AND CHALLENGES FOR IMPROVEMENTS

Health and Socio-economic developments are so closely intertwined that is impossible to achieve one without the other. While the economic development in India has been gaining momentum over the last decade, our health system is at crossroads today. Even though Government initiatives in public health have recorded some noteworthy successes over time (eradicate smallpox and Guineaworm, substantial decline in the number of Leprosy, Polio, and Malaria cases, etc.,[3] our achievements in health outcomes are only moderate by international standards; India is ranked 118 among 191 WHO member countries on overall health performance.[4] A few health statistics are worth mentioning:

Maternal death and disability

More than 100,000 mothers in India die every year, which amounts to one maternal death every five minutes. What is unfortunate is that more than 75 percent of these deaths are preventable if proper medical attention can be provided on time. And, for every maternal death, there are ten to 15 maternal disabilities, for lack of medical attention. What is the economic and social impact on maternal death and disability?

Infant and child mortality

An average IMR of 70 per 1,000 live births and a CMR of 95 per 1,000 live births are also very high compared with five to six CMR in developed nations.

Most of these deaths are also preventable.

HIV/AIDS

India with 5.1 million HIV/AIDS cases (official figures) has the highest number of HIV/AIDS cases as a country outside Africa. HIV/AIDS is hindering decades of health, economic and social progress. Indicators of human development – such as child mortality, literacy, and food production – are slipping as the disease ravages families, communities, economies, and health systems in heavily affected countries.

Non-communicable diseases

Non-communicable diseases are on the rise. According to a recent study on the burden of diseases in India,[5] the number of Cardiovascular diseases is expected to rise from the current level of 38 million in 2005 to 64 million by 2015, Diabetes from 30 million in 2005 to 45 million cases by 2015, and Cancer from 2 million in 2005 to 2.5 million cases by 2015.

Urban health

Urbanization is an important demographic shift worldwide. Today, nearly 50 percent of the world population is urban. India's urban population of 300 million represents 30 percent of our population. Government of India started urban health planning only ten years ago in the 9th Five Year Plan document.[6] An urban slum growth rate of 5 percent is causing serious concern for the civic and health authorities in municipalities and towns. Health of urban poor and its implications on the entire urban population should be analyzed and an appropriate urban health policy should be arrived at.

Environmental health

Contaminated water and poor sanitation is responsible for large proportion of diseases in India. Poor hygiene and sanitation account for 9 percent of all deaths and an estimated 27.4 million years of life are lost each year in India. Unfortunately in spite of such staggering ill health caused by poor hygiene and sanitation scant attention is being paid to its improvement. Currently only about 20 percent of rural households have toilets. The rate of increase of toilets in rural area is slow that it will take about 80 years to have 100 percent coverage in rural areas.[7] Given the situation in sanitation and hygiene is one of the urgent needs for improving rural health.

Healthcare insurance

The Government's contribution to the total healthcare expenditure is only 20 percent, and therefore out-of-pocket expenditure is as high as 80 percent. The cost of healthcare is increasing rapidly. A large majority of our population cannot afford healthcare expenses. In India, there are five forms of healthcare insurance/private insurance, social insurance, employer-provided cover, community insurance schemes, and government healthcare spend. Only 3-4 percent of population is insured. Insurance has grown by 100 percent in the last two years. It is estimated that about 160 million people will be covered by 2010, which is less than 15 percent of the population.

Support services

Support services such as blood banking, ambulance services, communication, medical-social work, hospital waste management, etc. are very essential to provide good quality of health and medical services. Indian healthcare sector lacks good support services. For example, there is a severe shortage of blood in many rural areas, ambulance service is unreliable and medical infection control and waste disposal are pathetic. In such a situation, it is very difficult to provide good quality and safe medical services. Thus improving support services should form an important agenda for improving healthcare delivery.

5.3 BUILDING HEALTH SYSTEMS

Building Health Systems that are responsive to community needs, particularly for the poor, requires politically difficult and administratively demanding choices

Health is a priority goal in its own right, as well as a central input into economic development and poverty reduction. The WHO Report on "Investing in Health for Economic Development",[8] suggests that for developing countries like India, health policies should focus on:

• Scaling up financial resources (e.g. public-private partnership).

• Tackling the non-financial obstacles in service delivery (e.g. logistics, HR, and governance issues).

The macroeconomic scenario of the Indian Health sector is not very encouraging. The total annual expenditure on Health is around Rs. 110,000 crores, and it accounts for 5.2 percent of our GDP. However, public health investment has declined from 1.3 percent of GDP to 0.9 percent by 2001 (comparable with China, Sri Lanka and Nepal are 2, 1.8 and 1.6 percent respectively). Government share of the total expenditure is only 17 percent, and therefore out-of-pocket expenditure is as high as 83 percent. Central contribution to overall public health spending in states is limited to 15 percent. Central budgetary allocation for health has remained static at 1.3 percent of the total central budget. State budgetary allocations have declined from 7 percent to less than 5.5 percent in many states. There is therefore an urgent need to scale up financial resources in the health sector.

Health is a state subject in India. However, many states do not have a clear health policy. The strategies of the states are mostly guided by the National Health Policy, and National Health Programs. There is no systematic effort at the state level to plan, and monitor the delivery of health services. Health services continue to be supply pushed than demand driven.

In short, managerial challenges are many to ensure availability, access, affordability, and equity in delivering health services to meet the community needs efficiently and effectively.

5.4 AVAILABILITY OF HEALTH SERVICES

Public health infrastructure

Between 1950 and 2000, the rural health infrastructure (SC/PHC/CHC) has gone up from 725 facilities to more than 163,000,[9] consisting of 4,000 rural sub district hospitals (called Community Health Centres-CHCs), 24,000 Primary Health Centres (PHCs), and 135,000 sub health Centres (SCs). Yet, there is a shortfall of 16 percent in the number of PHCs/SCs and as high as 58 percent in the case of CHCs.

Public health infrastructure is far from satisfactory as the delivery of services is hampered by several policy and management constraints,[10] of particular concerns being:

- Non-availability of staff.

- Weak referral system.

- Recurrent funding shortfalls.

- Lack of accountability for quality of care.

- Poor logistics management of supply of medicines and drugs.

All the above-mentioned concerns have been repeatedly mentioned in several meetings and documents for the past several years. Yet, the utilization of the massive public health infrastructure is abysmally low. Availability and access to public health facilities is very poor for women, children, and the socially disadvantaged sections of our society. The past unsatisfactory performance of our public health system in rural areas is forcing even the poor to seek healthcare from the private sector. The data shows that only 20 percent of outpatient and 45 percent for inpatient care is obtained from government health infrastructure while the rest is obtained from private sources.

Under RCH-II programme government is refocusing on primary and rural health services. It has decided to provide 24-hour services, seven days a week, in 50 percent of all PHCs over the next five years. Government has also decided to operationalize all designated first referral units in rural areas under RCH-II programme.

Private healthcare

The private sector is responding aggressively to meet the healthcare demands. Several studies have shown that people in general (rich or poor) have a preference to seek healthcare services from the private sector. Use of government facilities is mostly for indoor care, governed by the decisions on cost of care more than the quality (user perceptions).

Since the Government has not yet laid down any mandatory requirements for registering private healthcare facilities; it is very difficult to get reliable estimates of private health infrastructure in the country. Even though the scale of operations of the private sector is not clear, it is believed that private sector accounts for 67 percent of the total number of 30,000 hospitals and 33 percent of the total number of 1 million beds. Also, the private sector accounts for over 60 percent of the 5 million doctors in the country. Most of the services offered by the private sector are for secondary and tertiary care, and not much for preventive healthcare.

Based on the above estimates of public and private healthcare infrastructure, India has only about 100 beds per 100,000 populations against the WHO norms of 300 beds per 100,000. The number of doctors per 1,000 population is also well below the WHO norms. The demand supply gap is therefore large. Investment required to bridge the gap in the next ten years could range from Rs. 100,000 crore to Rs. 140,000 crore.[11] The sector can also create huge income and employment growth in ten years.

Affordability

As mentioned earlier, the utilization of public health facilities is only about 20 percent for outpatient services and 45 percent for inpatient care. In such a situation, poor people are forced to seek healthcare services from the private sector by paying high user fee. This partially explains our out-of-pocket expenditure on health at 80 percent.

Health Insurance is one option to address concerns on affordability. Regional licensing of health insurance business like in the US, and health insurance schemes like Yeshasvini, Arogya Bhagya Yojana, Arogya Bhadrata are worth exploring. A detailed analysis of the costs and benefits of the Employee State Insurance (ESI) scheme of the Ministry of Labor also would be helpful. The Government should facilitate the growth of private, social and community insurance to improve affordability.

Cost of care can also be contained if the service levels in public sector can be substantially improved, referral systems enforced and the unfinished agenda of controlling infectious diseases achieved.[12] The existing financing and payment systems are not suitable for countering market failures typical of insurance.

Insurance services without availability of reasonable quality healthcare service delivery will not serve the intended purpose.[13] It is necessary to ensure availability of health services for any insurance scheme to succeed.

Access

Availability of health infrastructure is only a necessary condition, but not sufficient, to guarantee delivery of services. Access to services is an equally important determinant in meeting the healthcare needs of people, especially those in rural areas. Ambulance services to transport the serious patients to referral centres are very minimal. Public transportation between PHC/CHC to the district/state hospitals is irregular and infrequent. Private transport is expensive. Many PHCs/CHCs do not even have telephones or wireless communications. The existing public health system in rural areas has therefore become very unreliable and undependable for access to healthcare facilities especially in emergencies.

Access to heath facilities is equally worse in some large towns and urban areas, since the heterogeneous urban population have different expectations from the urban health systems. Even though urban areas have more health facilities, and better transportation than rural areas, the location, operating time and other characteristics of public health facilities do not favor the urban slum populations accounting for 35-45 percent of urban population in India.

Telemedicine is being cited as an option worth exploring. Telemedicine infrastructure consists of a Telemedicine Specialist Centre (TSC) at a large hospital connected to a Telemedicine Consultation Centre (TCC) in a CHC/District hospital. Since 75 percent of all treatments do not require surgical interventions, telemedicine infrastructure can theoretically address 75 percent of our healthcare needs. Telemedicine infrastructure can also support Continuing Medical Education (CME) for professional development of doctors, as well as facilitate health promotion activities. Indian Space Research Organization (ISRO) is playing a vital role by providing VSAT connectivity for telemedicine centres.

Effective use of regular and mobile telephone can also improve access and quality of healthcare in rural areas. Example, a PHC/CHC doctor can consult a specialist on phone at a district Head quarters or in a medical college.

Equity

Over and above availability, access, and affordability concerns, a fourth determinant of the quality of healthcare services focuses on equity of services.

In the period when centralized planning was accepted as a key instrument of development in the country, the attainment of an equitable distribution was considered one of the main objectives. Despite this conscious focus in the development process, the attainment of health status differs significantly across states as shown in National Health Policy (2003).

While inequality exists between low-high performing states, as well as between populations with different socio-economic status, inequality concerns between the rural and urban areas are of a different nature. The dimensions of equity assume larger proportions in urban areas because of socio-economic and cultural diversity of urban population. Indian population growth is characterized by the 2-3-4-5 syndrome: overall population growth at 2 percent, urban population growth at 3 percent, mega cities growth at 4 percent, and slum population growth at 5 percent. Equity concerns in urban health have to address these realities as well.

Health insurance, mentioned earlier, can also address equity concerns. With greater coverage through insurance, equity in healthcare will improve through effective cross subsidization.

Health sector reforms

Health sector is complex with multiple goals, multiple products, and different beneficiaries[14] describes health sector reform as "sustained, purposeful change to improve the efficiency, equity, and effectiveness of the health sector". The implementation of large-scale health system reform demands political sensitivity, strategic thinking and management capacity of a high order. In practice, the application of health system reforms takes a wide variety of shapes by combining different components into different configurations.

The Indian public health system has so far remained largely unaffected by the appetite for large-scale reform affecting so may other countries, and thereby has avoided many of the pitfalls, which early reformers experienced. Experience of nine states in India, which undertook health sector reforms are well documented.[15] India is well placed now to profit from others' experience and to develop a uniquely Indian set of reforms to enable the health system better to meet the increasing expectations of its users and staff. The second advantage India has are the highly competent professionals and reputed management institutes that can provide technical support to the reform efforts by rigorously analyzing the experiences and ongoing efforts. The third advantage India has in health reform is that the economic reforms started in 1991 have yielded good results thus creating a positive political and social environment for public system reforms in general. Above all, the Government of India has demonstrated political will to improve the delivery of health services in our goal for greater socio economic development.

Below we illustrate a sample of three major reforms successfully implemented in India in two Indian States, namely, Tamil Nadu, Madhya Pradesh, and Andhra Pradesh. It should be realized that replication of these reform initiatives on a nation-wide scale needs careful planning and political commitment.

The above paragraphs have given the required and general information about the history of health services in India and different types of it. But such information will become more transparent by bringing in the example of Mysore as case study. In the following, the scholar tries to bring-forth the detailed information about the status of health care system in Mysore as the exact information is available from first hand data. Mysore case will particularly clarify the status of health system that can be generalized to other parts of Karnataka and India with little consideration.

5.5 HEALTH IN KARNATAKA

Karnataka state has a total area of 191,791 km^2 and 8th largest state. The state has 30 administrative districts with a total population of 611 lakhs (*Census, 2011*) of which 51% are male and 49% are female. It is the 9th most populous state having a population density of 319 per sq. km. The sex ratio is 968 (females per 1000 males). The total literacy rate is 75.60% (male – 82.85%, and of female – 68.13%). Almost 34% of the total population in the state lives in urban areas. The State's MMR of 178 *(SRS 07-09)* is the highest amongst the Southern States. The IMR of 41 *(SRS 2009)* has reduced from 52 *(SRS 2003)*. Karnataka has a TFR of 2.0 (*SRS 2009)* and it has achieved the national TFR target (of 2.1 by the year 2012). There are 176 sub-divisions/taluks and 176 blocks and 29240 villages, Out of 30 districts in Karnataka, 7 are high focus districts (Bellary, Bidar, Chamarajanagar, Chitradurga, Davangere, Kolar and Raichur). The State has designated 7 'C' category districts based on vulnerability mapping i.e. Bijapur, Bidar, Gulbarga, Yadgir, Koppal, Bagalkote, Raichur. The following public health infrastructures are available in its 30 districts.

Table 5.1: Status of public health facilities

Public health facilities	Present	Required	Remarks
District hospitals	30	30	No. of DH required (1 per district)
Sub-divisional hospitals	84 (other than CHC at or above block level but below district level)	146	
Community centers (Health)	186		
Primary health centers	2175	1862	@ 1 PHC/30,000 population excluding 8 cities having above 1
Health sub-centers	9236	9066	@ 1 HSC/5000 population excluding 8 cities having population above 1 lakh

Source: NRHM State-wise progress, June 2012
As per provisional infrastructure/HRH gap analysis, September 2012 (NHSRC)

5.6 GENERATION OF HUMAN RESOURCES FOR HEALTH

There is still a gap in the production of HRH in the state in both public and private sectors resulting in low HRH availability pool in the market for recruitment.

Table 5.2: Availability of medical, nursing /allied professional institutes (government & private) in Karnataka

Sl. No.	Type of Institute	Type of sector			Annual intake		
		Govt.	Private	Total	Govt.	Private	Total
1	ANMTCs	14	31	45	420	905	1325
2	GNM schools (diploma in nursing)	127	420	547	421	24537	24958
3	Nursing colleges (B.Sc.)	6	334	340	410	17873	18283
4	B.Sc. in Medical Laboratory Technology (BMLT)	16	16				
5	Ayurvedha (BAMS)+	60	60				
6	Medical Colleges (MBBS)/ Diploma seats – Anesthesia/(O&G)	11/ 5/4	32/ 20/19	43/ 25/23	1350/ 28/29	4655/ 70/72	6005/ 98/101

*private includes trust, municipal, corporation etc; **As per NCI/MCI, Dec'2012*

Each year, 6005 MBBS graduates are produced in the state. The state runs 11 government medical colleges offering MBBS degrees having 1350 annual seats in 10 districts.

Table 5.3: Lists of government medical colleges having MBBS course along with annual intake in Karnataka

Name of Medical colleges	Annual Intake
Bangalore Medical College and Research Institute, Bangalore	250
Belgaum Institute of Medical Sciences, Belgaum	100
Bidar Institute of Medical Sciences, Bidar	100
ESI Medical college, Bangalore	100
Government Medical College, Mysore	150
Hassan Institute of Medical Sciences, Hassan	100
Karnataka Institute of Medical Sciences, Hubli	150
Madhya Institute of Medical Sciences, Madhya	100
Raichur Institute of Medical Sciences, Raichur	100
Shimoga Institute of Medical Sciences, Shimoga	100
Bijaynagar Institute of Medical Sciences, Bellary	100
Total	**1350**

Source: NRHM State-wise progress, June 2012
As per provisional infrastructure/HRH gap analysis, September 2012 (NHSRC)

5.7 DEPLOYMENT OF HUMAN RESOURCES IN HEALTH

Karnataka does not face much shortage of human resources for health in any categories of health service providers. The number of posts that are sanctioned does not aligned to the staffing pattern as per recommendations of IPHS. The GDMO are recruited through direct appointment after interviews. There is direct appointment and promotion for specialist (regular) from 2012 (March). There were 600 vacant posts of specialists; against which 275 had applied and only 75 reported for joining the public service.

For example, there are only 7810 sanctioned posts of staff nurses against the 2589 sanctioned posts of medical officers which are more or less as per the standard norms of 3 nurses per 1 doctor recommended by the WHO. There were no contractual appointments under NRHM in period from 2008-2011 as per order of Supreme Court. The current status of key categories of staff in public health system is given in the following table.

There is Special Recruitment Committee (SRC) established in Department of Health & Family Welfare to speed up the recruitment process for doctors through direct recruitment. This process of recruitment usually takes 3-6 months. The recruitments of GDMO and specialists is done through SRC. In the recruitment year for 2009-10; only 60% of MBBS doctors actually joined the public service.

There has been delay in conducting interviews/tests and offering the appointment letters etc due to reasons i.e. court directives, assembly sessions, election code of conduct etc. Of the number of GDMO selected, 60% reported for duty and 40% did not report at all. As for the specialists, hardly 20% reported for service while 80% of specialists did not report. Among the paramedical, almost 90% joined the service. The promotions given are time bound in nature after serving a period of 6 years, 13 years and 20 years in service for medical officers. In March, 2012; 328 doctors (specialists) joined the service. As on 31st of January, 2013; there were 122 surgeons (R) and 274 gynecologists (R) working in the state against sanctioned posts of 231 surgeons and 512 gynecologists' posts. Only diploma holders applied for GDMO and 35 of such diploma holders work as specialists for post of GDMO.

There are 2nd ANM with qualification of staff nurse working under NRHM in contractual appointments with a salary of Rs. 10,000/- per month.

Table 5.4: Status of key staff categories in public health system in Karnataka

District	Pharmacist		Lab technician		Radio-grapher		LHV		Staff nurses		ANM		Regular MO	
	San	Vac	San	Vac	San	Vac	San	Vac	San	Vac	San	Vac	San	Vac
Bagalkote	78	12	78	24	2	1	-	-	168	12	255	65	66	20
Bangalore Urban	111	4	145	77	6	3	-	-	437	108	354	99	134	51
Bangalore Rural	60	2	43	14	-	-	-	-	85	61	261	100	60	14
Belgaum	192	53	157	46	-	-	-	-	287	68	718	313	175	68
Bellary	92	32	77	32	-	-	-	-	184	77	422	186	120	47
Bidar	71	19	59	4	-	-	-	-	92	48	287	21	97	29
Bijapur	97	16	88	30	1	1	-	-	253	47	319	97	93	34
Chamaraja-nagar	75	48	73	31	-	-	-	-	117	7	266	61	79	12
Chikkaballapura	79	16	59	29	-	-	-	-	152	60	318	175	81	23
Chikmagalur	114	59	82	20	2	1	-	-	246	81	380	97	128	46
Chitradurga	115	39	86	22	-	-	-	-	277	93	380	129	122	65
Darshina Kannada	94	60	80	16	-	-	-	-	140	21	452	103	96	33
Davanagere	119	29	79	8	-	-	-	-	156	21	362	116	127	26
Dharwad	45	2	42	7	1	-	-	-	134	6	220	28	52	13
Gadag	53	6	51	16	-	-	-	-	126	25	194	61	46	23
Gulbarga	129	59	95	45	-	-	-	-	379	163	413	253	178	86
Hassan	177	98	131	53	2	2	-	-	323	128	653	340	228	102
Haveri	95	21	68	19	-	-	-	-	186	101	324	89	79	25
Kodagu	60	41	53	26	-	-	-	-	193	26	243	49	52	23
Kolar	89	27	74	37	2	2	-	-	254	76	327	137	87	22
Koppal	68	26	63	28	-	-	-	-	149	46	185	55	57	25
Mandya	158	54	98	18	-	-	-	-	213	49	431	100	165	31
Mysore	177	89	118	48	-	-	-	-	255	99	813	408	189	49
Raichur	68	22	60	14	-	-	-	-	127	22	230	74	69	26
Ramanagara	75	10	55	12	-	-	-	-	124	29	252	99	71	5
Shimoga	121	36	108	53	2	-	-	-	234	105	407	165	160	59
Tumkur	181	37	134	30	1	-	-	-	316	106	589	166	166	33
Udupi	85	33	78	16	1	-	-	-	137	26	327	76	77	18
Uttara Kannada	110	43	96	46	2	1	-	-	226	29	383	49	113	60
Yadgir	60	24	58	25	1	1	-	-	115	44	178	96	61	18
Total	**3048**	**1017**	**2488**	**846**	**23**	**12**	**0**	**0**	**6085**	**1784**	**10943**	**3807**	**3228**	**1086**

Source: NRHM State-wise progress, June 2012
As per provisional infrastructure/HRH gap analysis, September 2012 (NHSRC)

Table 5.5: Status of staff nurse, ANM and LT in Karnataka (April-June,2012)

Name of district	Staff nurse				ANM				LT			
	S	R	C	V	S	R	C	V	S	R	C	V
Bagalkote	168	-	168	12	255	-	30	65	78	-	5	24
Bangalore Urban	85	-	60	61	261	-	5	603	43	-	4	14
Bangalore Rural	437	-	131	108	354	-	0	134	145	-	3	77
Belgaum	287	-	333	68	718	-	16	100	157	-	11	46
Bellary	184	-	217	77	422	-	60	189	77	-	7	32
Bidar	92	-	171	48	287	-	9	21	59	-	6	4
Bijapur	253	-	147	47	319	-	30	97	88	-	6	30
Chamarajanagar	117	-	124	7	266	-	20	61	73	-	3	31
Chikkaballapura	152	-	82	60	318	-	39	175	59	-	2	29
Chikmagalur	246	-	104	81	380	-	33	97	82	-	2	20
Chitradurga	277	-	129	93	380	-	49	129	86	-	6	22
Darshina Kannada	140	-	167	21	452	-	37	103	80	-	6	16
Davanagere	156	-	75	21	362	-	0	116	79	-	5	8
Dharwad	134	-	72	6	220	-	4	28	42	-	3	7
Gadag	126	-	104	25	194	-	11	61	51	-	5	16
Gulbarga	379	-	281	163	413	-	55	253	95	-	6	45
Hassan	323	-	149	128	653	-	69	340	131	-	3	53
Haveri	186	-	152	101	324	-	10	89	68	-	7	19
Kodagu	193	-	49	26	243	-	3	49	53	-	5	26
Kolar	254	-	162	76	327	-	24	137	74	-	5	37
Koppal	149	-	171	46	185	-	35	55	63	-	11	28
Mandya	213	-	109	49	431	-	44	100	98	-	4	18
Mysore	255	-	107	99	813	-	9	408	118	-	0	48
Raichur	127	-	178	22	230	-	76	74	60	-	8	14
Ramanagara	124	-	75	29	252	-	16	99	55	-	4	12
Shimoga	234	-	119	105	407	-	70	165	108	-	4	53
Tumkur	316	-	189	106	589	-	13	166	134	-	4	30
Udupi	137	-	48	26	327	-	60	76	78	-	4	16
Uttara Kannada	226	-	94	29	383	-	0	49	96	-	5	46
Yadgir	115	-	143	44	178	-	73	96	58	-	5	25
Total	6085		4110	1784	10943		900	4135	2488		149	846

Source: NRHM State-wise progress, June 2012
As per provisional infrastructure/HRH gap analysis, September 2012 (NHSRC)

Table 5.6: Status of key staff categories in public health system in Karnataka

Category of staff		Number of posts		
Key	Sub	Sanctioned	In-position ®	Vacant
Specialists	Pediatrician	211	87	124
	Gynecologist	512	388	124
	Surgeon	231	129	102
	Anesthetist	201	176	25
	Physician	379	163	216
	Ophthalmologist	176	106	70
	Orthopedics	181	147	34
	Psychiatrist	22	17	5
	ENT Specialist	129	84	45
Medical Officer	GDMO	2586	2297®+85©=2382	289
Dental Officer	Dental Health Officer	245	183®	62
Nursing superintendent		69	56®	13
Staff nurse		7810	6730®	1080
LHV		1432	1050®	382
Lab technician		2197	1644®	553
Pharmacist		2691	2133®	558
MPW (Male)		5810	3500®	2310
MPW (Female)		10025	8773®	1252
Total		34907	34907	7244

Source: ROP-Karnataka (2012-13); ® refers to regular appointments

Table 5.7: Staff position of specialists in various hospitals in DHS as on 6.7.2012

Specialists	Sanctioned post	In-position ®	Vacant
Chief Medical Officer/Surgeon	130	104	26
General medicine	379	163	216
General surgeon	231	129	102
Obstetrician and Gynecologist	512	388	124
Anesthetist	201	176	25
Pediatrician	211	87	124
Ophthalmologist	176	106	70
Orthopediatrician	181	147	34
ENT surgeon	129	84	45
Dermatologist	66	14	52
Psychiatrist	22	17	5
Radiologist	60	34	26
Pathologist	20	18	2
Family medicine	11	6	5
Microbiologist	15	14	1
Bio-chemistry	9	7	2
BB	23	18	5
TB	19	17	2
Nephrologists	261	6	20
Plastic surgeon	12	1	11
Cardiologist	6	4	2
Total	2674	1540	899

Source: ROP-Karnataka (2012-13); ® refers to regular appointments

Table 5.8: District-wise lists of specialist/SMO, Sr. Specialist/DCMO for the sanctioned posts, working (in-position) and vacancy posts/ percentage in Karnataka (as on 9th July, 2012)

Name of district	Sanctioned posts	In-position ®	Vacant
Bagalkote	104	47/4	57
Bangalore Urban	46	45/2	1
Bangalore Rural	170	163/1	7
Belgaum	164	74/3	90
Bellary	124	68/1	56
Bidar	76	41/2	35
Bijapur	101	38/0	63
Chamarajanagar	56	39/0	17
Chikkaballapura	79	51/2	28
Chikmagalur	56	39/0	17
Chitradurga	115	68/1	47
Davanagere	116	89/1	27
Dharwad	51	21/3	30
Gadag	64	22/2	42
Gulbarga	165	86/3	79
Hassan	125	75/0	50
Haveri	94	46/1	48
Kodagu	89	62/0	27
Kolar	106	84/0	22
Koppal	83	39/0	44
Mandya	84	70/2	14
Mysore	122	109/0	13
Raichur	65	30/2	35
Ramanagara	67	54/2	13
Shimoga	106	73/1	33
Tumkur	152	116/2	36
Udupi	60	37/1	23
Uttara Kannada	147	95/8	52
Yadagiri	54	26/3	28
Total	2841	1940/52=1992	1034

Source: Public Health Workforce in Karnataka: Issues and Challenges. (2013). New Delhi: Ministry of Health and Family Welfare, Government of India.

Deployment of Specialists/Trained MOs

There is not much shortage of specialists in the state. 63% of the specialists (regular) are in position against the sanctioned number of specialists in the state as in July, 2012. If we also add the contractual appointments for posts of specialists; it increased to 66% respectively. The deployment of specialists and trained MOs is more or rational in one of the district i.e. Tumkur. There are 9 designated FRUs (GH/SHDs) across Tumkur district. Out of 20 sanctioned posts of O&G across these 9 FRUs (GH/SDHs); 16 were in-position and out of 9 sanctioned posts of anesthetists, 9 were in position and out of 9 sanctioned posts of pediatrician; 6 were in position respectively. In addition, there are 2 EmOCs and 2 LSAS trained Medical Officers.

Table 5.9: Number of designated FRUs, deployment of specialist/DGMO/ trained MO in Tumkur district

Name of district	Number of designated FRU	Functional till Dec'2012	No. of FRU where ≥1 specialist (A/P/G)/trained MO-T are posted
Tumkur	9		Out of 20 sanctioned posts of O&G; 16 were in-position; out of 9 sanctioned posts of anesthetist, 9 were in position; out of 9 sanctioned posts of pediatrician; 6 were in position
Total FRUs in the state	**192**		

Source: Public Health Workforce in Karnataka: Issues and Challenges. (2013). New Delhi: Ministry of Health and Family Welfare, Government of India.

120

Table 5.10: Break up of appointments as regular and contractual for various service providers

Staff category	Sanction posts	In-position		
		Regular	Contractual	Total
Specialist	3007	1940	52	1992
GDMO/MO	2586	2297	85	2382
Staff nurse	7810	6730	4110	10840
ANM	10025	8773	900	9673
LT	2197	1644	149	1793

Source: Public Health Workforce in Karnataka: Issues and Challenges. (2013). New Delhi: Ministry of Health and Family Welfare, Government of India.

5.8 TRAININGS AND CAPACITY BUILDING

For pre-service trainings, Karnataka has adequate number of medical colleges, nursing and ANM schools run by government and private sector. The Nursing schools in Karnataka are under Department of Medical Education. The State has more than required number of staff nurses. The State has 28 ANM training schools run by the government and 30 schools run by private. Each of the Government ANM School takes up a batch of approx 30 (3 tribal ANMTCs have 40 seats) every year. The SIHFW (State Institute of Health and Family Welfare) is the main training center in the state. It has helped in making the comprehensive training plan for Karnataka. This plan incorporates all the training under RCH and other health programmes which have been incorporated in the PIP as well. Out of 12 key faculty positions (of Director's levels) including the Director, only 5 had been filled up. There are three consultants for monitoring of training activities under RCH. It is the nodal agency for all the in-service trainings under NRHM. The faculty and staff positions of SIHFW are currently understaffed as given in the following table.

Table 5.11: Faculty positions at SIHFW, Karnataka and at 19 DTCs

Designation of post	Sanctioned	Occupied	Vacant
Director	1	1	0
Joint Director	1	0	1
Deputy Director	10	4	6
Assistant Administrative Officer	1	1	0
Accounts Officer	1	1	0
Accounts Superintendent	1	0	1
FDA	2	2	0
SDA	2	2	0
Steno	2	1	1
Typist	2	1	1
Drivers	5	3	2
Group D	8	8	0
Principal	19	18	1
Health Education Officer	19	6	13
District Nursing Officers	19	6	13
First Division Assistants	19	16	3
Second Division Assistants	19	12	7
Drivers	19	7	12
Group D	38	31	7
House-keeping	38	26	12

Source: Public Health Workforce in Karnataka: Issues and Challenges. (2013). New Delhi: Ministry of Health and Family Welfare, Government of India.

Health Insurance

Health insurance in a narrow sense would be 'an individual or group purchasing health care coverage in advance by paying a fee called *premium*.' In its broader sense, it would be any arrangement that helps to defer, delay, reduce or altogether avoid payment for health care incurred by individuals *Regional Overview in South-East Asia Page 82* and households. Given the appropriateness of this definition in the Indian context, this is the definition, we would adopt. The health insurance market in India is very limited covering about 10% of the total population. The existing schemes can be categorized as:

(1) Voluntary health insurance schemes or private-for-profit schemes;

(2) Employer-based schemes;

(3) Insurance offered by NGOs/community based health insurance, and

(4) Mandatory health insurance schemes or government run schemes (namely ESIS, CGHS).

Voluntary health insurance schemes or private-for-profit schemes

In private insurance, buyers are willing to pay premium to an insurance company that pools people with similar risks and insures them for health expenses. The key distinction is that the premiums are set at a level, which provides a profit to third party and provider institutions. Premiums are based on an assessment of the risk status of the consumer (or of the group of employees) and the level of benefits provided, rather than as a proportion of the consumer's income. In the public sector, the General Insurance Corporation (GIC) and its four subsidiary companies (National Insurance Corporation, New India Assurance Company, Oriental Insurance Company and United Insurance Company) and the Life Insurance Corporation (LIC) of India provide voluntary insurance schemes. The Life Insurance Corporation offers *Ashadeep Plan II and Jeevan Asha Plan II*. The General Insurance Corporation offers Personal Accident policy, *Jan Arogya policy, Raj Rajeshwari policy, Mediclaim policy, Overseas Mediclaim policy, Cancer Insurance policy, Bhavishya Arogya policy* and *Dreaded Disease policy.*[16]

Of the various schemes offered, Mediclaim is the main product of the GIC. The Medical Insurance Scheme or Mediclaim was introduced in November 1986 and it covers individuals and groups with persons aged 5–80 yrs. Children (3 months-5 years) are covered with their parents. This scheme provides for reimbursement of medical expenses (now offers cashless scheme) by an individual towards hospitalization and domiciliary *Social Health Insurance Page 83* hospitalization as per the sum insured. There are exclusions and pre-existing disease clauses. Premiums are calculated based on age and the sum insured, which in turn varies from Rs 15,000 to Rs 5,00,000. In 1995/96 about half a million Mediclaim policies were issued with about 1.8 million beneficiaries. The coverage for the year 2000-01 was around 7.2 million.

Another scheme, namely the *Jan Arogya Bima* policy specifically targets the poor population groups. It also covers reimbursement of hospitalization costs up to Rs 5 000 annually for an individual premium of Rs 100 a year. The same exclusion mechanisms apply for this scheme as those under the Mediclaim policy. A family discount of 30% is granted, but there is no group discount or agent commission. However, like the Mediclaim, this policy too has had only limited success. The *Jan Arogya Bima* Scheme had only covered 400,000 individuals by 1997.

The year 1999 marked the beginning of a new era for health insurance in the Indian context. With the passing of the Insurance Regulatory Development

Authority Bill (IRDA) the insurance sector was opened to private and foreign participation, thereby paving the way for the entry of private health insurance companies. The Bill also facilitated the establishment of an authority to protect the interests of the insurance holders by regulating, promoting and ensuring orderly growth of the insurance industry. The bill allows foreign promoters to hold paid up capital of up to 26 percent in an Indian company and requires them to have a capital of Rs 100 crore along with a business plan to begin its operations. Currently, a few companies such as Bajaj Alliance, ICICI, Royal Sundaram, and Cholamandalam among others are offering health insurance schemes. The nature of schemes offered by these companies is described briefly.

Bajaj Allianz: Bajaj Alliance offers three health insurance schemes namely, Health Guard, Critical Illness Policy and Hospital Cash Daily Allowance Policy.

- The Health Guard scheme is available to those aged 5 to 75 years (not allowing entry for those over 55 years of age), with the sum assured ranging from Rs 1,000,000 to 500,000. It offers cashless benefit and medical reimbursement for hospitalization expenses (pre and post-hospitalization) at various hospitals across India (subject to *Regional Overview in South-East Asia Page 84* exclusions and conditions). In case the member opts for hospitals besides the empanelled ones, the expenses incurred by him are reimbursed within 14 working days from submission of all the documents. While pre-existing diseases are excluded at the time of taking the policy, they are covered from the 5th year onwards if the policy is continuously renewed for four years and the same has been declared while taking the policy for the first time. Other discounts and benefits like tax exemption, health check-up at end of four claims free year, etc. can be availed of by the insured.

- The Critical Illness policy pays benefits in case the insured is diagnosed as suffering from any of the listed critical events and survives for minimum of 30 days from the date of diagnosis. The illnesses covered include: first heart attack; Coronary artery disease requiring surgery: stroke; cancer; kidney failure; major organ transplantation; multiple sclerosis; surgery on aorta; primary pulmonary arterial hypertension, and paralysis. While exclusion clauses apply, premium rates are competitive and high-sum insurance can be opted for by the insured.

- The Hospital Cash Daily Allowance Policy provides cash benefit for each and every completed day of hospitalization, due to sickness or accident. The amount payable per day is dependant on the selected scheme. Dependant spouse and children (aged 3 months – 21 years) can also be covered under the Policy. The benefits payable to the dependants are linked to that of insured. The Policy pays for a maximum single hospitalization period of 30 days and an overall hospitalization period of 30/60 completed days per policy period per person regardless of the number of confinements to hospital/nursing home per policy period.

ICICI Lombard: ICICI Lombard offers Group Health Insurance Policy. This policy is available to those aged 5 – 80 years, (with children being covered with their parents) and is given to corporate bodies, institutions, and associations. The sum insured is minimum Rs 15 000/- and a maximum of Rs 500 000/-. The premium chargeable depends upon the age of the person and the sum insured selected. A slab wise group discount is admissible if the group size exceeds 100. The policy covers reimbursement of hospitalization expenses incurred for diseases *Social Health Insurance Page 85* contracted or injuries sustained in India. Medical expenses up to 30 days for Pre-hospitalization and up to 60 days for post-hospitalization are also admissible. Exclusion clauses apply. Moreover, favourable claims experience is recognized by discount and conversely, unfavourable claims experience attracts loading on renewal premium. On payment of additional premium, the policy can be extended to cover maternity benefits, pre-existing diseases, and reimbursement of cost of health check-up after four consecutive claims-free years.

Royal Sundaram Group: The *Shakthi* Health Shield policy offered by the Royal Sundaram group can be availed by members of the women's group, their spouses and dependent children. No age limits apply. The premium for adults aged up to 45 years is Rs. 125 per year, for those aged more than 45 years is Rs. 175 per year. Children are covered at Rs 65 per year. Under this policy, hospital benefits up to Rs. 7,000 per annum can be availed, with a limit per claim of Rs. 5,000. Other benefits include maternity benefit of Rs. 3,000 subject to waiting period of nine months after first enrolment and for first two children only. Exclusion clauses apply.[17]

Cholamandalam General Insurance: The benefits offered (in association with the Paramount Health Care, a re-insurer) in case of an illness or accident resulting in hospitalization, are cash-free hospitalization in more than 1,400 hospitals across India, reimbursement of the expenses during pre- hospitalization

(60 days prior to hospitalization) and post- hospitalization (90 days after discharge) stages of treatment. Over 130 minor surgeries that require less than 24 hours hospitalization under day care procedure are also covered. Extra health covers like general health and eye examination, local ambulance service, hospital daily allowance, and 24 hours assistance can be availed of. Exclusion clauses apply.

Employer-based schemes Employers in both the public and private sector offers employer-based insurance schemes through their own employer-managed facilities by way of lump sum payments, reimbursement of employee's health expenditure for outpatient care and hospitalization, fixed medical allowance, monthly or annual irrespective of actual expenses, or covering them under the group health insurance policy. The railways, defence and security forces, plantations *Regional Overview in South-East Asia Page 86* sector and mining sector provide medical services and/or benefits to its own employees. The population coverage under these schemes is minimal, about 30-50 million people.

Insurance offered by NGOs/community-based health insurance Community-based funds refer to schemes where members prepay a set amount each year for specified services. The premia are usually flat rate (not income-related) and therefore not progressive. Making profit is not the purpose of these funds, but rather improving access to services. Often there is a problem with adverse selection because of a large number of high-risk members, since premiums are not based on assessment of individual risk status. Exemptions may be adopted as a means of assisting the poor, but this will also have adverse effect on the ability of the insurance fund to meet the cost of benefits.

Community-based schemes are typically targeted at poorer populations living in communities, in which they are involved in defining contribution level and collecting mechanisms, defining the content of the benefit package, and / or allocating the schemes, financial resources.[18] Such schemes are generally run by trust hospitals or nongovernmental organizations (NGOs). The benefits offered are mainly in terms of preventive care, though ambulatory and in-patient care is also covered. Such schemes tend to be financed through patient collection, government grants and donations. Increasingly in India, CBHI schemes are negotiating with the profit insured respondents for purchase of custom designed group insurance policies. However, the coverage of such schemes is low, covering about 30-50 million.[19] A review by Bennett, Cresse et al.[20] indicates that many community-based insurance schemes suffer from poor design and management, fail to include the poorest-of-the poor, have low membership and require extensive financial support. Other issues relate to sustainability and replication of such schemes.

Self-Employed Women's Association (SEWA), Gujarat: This scheme established in 1992, provides health, life and assets insurance to women working in the informal sector and their families. The enrolment in the year 2002 was 93,000. This scheme operates in collaboration with the National Insurance Company (NIC). Under SEWA's most popular policy, a premium of Rs 85 per individual is paid by the woman for life, health and assets insurance. At an additional payment of Rs 55, her husband too can be covered. Rs 20 per member is then paid to the National Insurance Company (NIC) which provides coverage to a maximum of Rs 2,000 per person per year for hospitalization. After being hospitalized at a hospital of one's choice (public or private), the insurance claim is submitted to SEWA. The responsibility for enrolment of members, for processing and approving of claims rests with SEWA. NIC in turn receives premiums from SEWA annually and pays them a lumpsum on a monthly basis for all claims reimbursed.

Another CBHI scheme located in Gujarat, is that run by the **Tribhuvandas Foundation (TF),** Anand. This was established in 2001, with the membership being restricted to members of the AMUL Dairy Cooperatives. Since then, over 1,00,000 households have been enrolled under this scheme, with the TF functioning as a third party insurer.

The Mallur Milk Cooperative in Karnataka established a CBHI scheme in 1973. It covers 7 000 people in three villages and outpatient and inpatient health care are directly provided.

A similar scheme was established in 1972 at **Sewagram,** Wardha in Maharashtra. This scheme covers about 14 390 people in 12 villages and members are provided with outpatient and inpatient care directly by Sewagram.

The **Action for Community Organization, Rehabilitation and Development (ACCORD),** Nilgiris, Tamil Nadu was established in 1991. Around 13 000 *Adivasis* (tribals) are covered under a group policy purchased from New India Assurance.

Another scheme located in Tamil Nadu is **Kadamalai Kalanjia Vattara Sangam (KKVS),** Madurai. This was established in 2000 and covers members of women's self-help groups and their families. Its enrolment in 2002 was around 5 710, with the KKVS functioning as a third party insurer.

The Voluntary Health Services (VHS), Chennai, Tamil Nadu was established in 1963. It offers sliding premium with free care to the poorest. The benefits include discounted rates on both outpatient and inpatient care, with the VHS functioning as both insurer and health care provider. In 1995, its membership was 124 715. However, this scheme suffers from low levels of cost recovery due to problems of adverse selection.

Raigarh Ambikapur Health Association (RAHA), Chhatisgarh was established in 1972, and functions as a third party administrator. Its membership in the year 1993 was 72,000.

Social Insurance or mandatory health insurance schemes or government run schemes (namely the ESIS, CGHS) Social insurance is an earmarked fund set up by government with explicit benefits in return for payment. It is usually compulsory for certain groups in the population and the premiums are determined by income (and hence ability to pay) rather than related to health risk. The benefit packages are standardized and contributions are earmarked for spending on health services The government-run schemes include the Central Government Health Scheme (CGHS) and the Employees State Insurance Scheme (ESIS).

Reproduced from Mahal A (2001), 'Assessing Private Health Insurance in India: Potential Impacts and Regulatory Issues', Discussion Paper Series, No. 16, National Council of Applied Economic Research, New Delhi. p. 35 *Regional Overview in South-East Asia Page 92.*

Central Government Health Scheme (CGHS) Since 1954, all employees of the Central Government (present and retired); some autonomous and semi-government organizations, MPs, judges, freedom fighters and journalists are covered under the Central Government Health Scheme (CGHS). This scheme was designed to replace the cumbersome and expensive system of reimbursements.[21] It aims at providing comprehensive medical care to the Central Government employees and the benefits offered include all outpatient facilities, and preventive and promotive care in dispensaries. Inpatient facilities in government hospitals and approved private hospitals are also covered. This scheme is mainly funded through Central Government funds, with premiums ranging from Rs 15 to Rs 150 per month based on salary scales. The coverage of this scheme has grown substantially with provision for the non-allopathic systems of medicine as well as for allopathy. Beneficiaries at this moment are around 432,000, spread across 22 cities. The CGHS has been criticized from the point of view of quality and accessibility. Subscribers have complained of high out-of-pocket expenses due to slow reimbursement and incomplete coverage for private health care (as only 80% of cost is reimbursed if referral is made to private facility when such facilities are not available with the CGHS).

Employee and State Insurance Scheme (ESIS) The enactment of the Employees State Insurance Act in 1948 led to formulation of the Employees State Insurance Scheme. This scheme provides protection to employees against loss of wages due to inability to work due to sickness, maternity, disability and death due to employment injury. It offers medical and cash benefits, preventive and promotive care and health education. Medical care is also provided to employees and their family members without fee for service. Originally, the ESIS scheme covered all power-using non-seasonal factories employing 10 or more people. Later, it was extended to cover employees working in all non-power using factories with 20 or more persons. While persons working in mines and plantations, or an organization offering health benefits as good as or better than ESIS, are specifically excluded. Service establishments like shops, hotels, restaurants, cinema houses, road transport and news papers printing are now covered. The monthly wage limit for enrolment in the ESIS is Rs. 6 500, with a prepayment contribution in the form of a payroll tax of 1.75% by employees, 4.75% of employees' wages to be paid by the employers, and 12.5% of the total expenses are borne by the state governments. The number of beneficiaries is over 33 million spread over 620 ESI centres across states. Under the ESIS, there were 125 hospitals, 42 annexes and 1 450 dispensaries with over 23 000 beds facilities. The scheme is managed and financed by the Employees State Insurance Corporation (a public undertaking) through the state governments, with total expenditure of Rs 3 300 million or Rs 400/- per capita insured person. The ESIS programme has attracted considerable criticism. A report based on patient surveys conducted in Gujarat[22] found that over half of those covered did not seek care from ESIS facilities. Unsatisfactory nature of ESIS services, low quality drugs, long waiting periods, impudent behaviour of personnel, lack of interest or low interest on part of employees and low awareness of ESI procedures, were some of the reasons cited.

Other Government Initiatives Apart from the government-run schemes, social security benefits for the disadvantaged groups can be availed of, under the provisions of the Maternity Benefit (Amendment) Act 1995, Workmen's Compensation (Amendment) Act 1984, Plantation Labour Act 1951, Mine Mines Labour Welfare Fund Act 1946, *Beedi* Workers Welfare Fund Act 1976 and Building and other Construction Workers (Regulation of Employment and Conditions of Service) Act, 1996. The Government of India has also undertaken initiatives to address issues relating to access to public health systems especially for the vulnerable sections of the society. The National Health Policy 2002 acknowledges this and aims to evolve a policy structure, which reduces such inequities and allows the disadvantaged sections of the population a fairer access to public health services. Ensuring more equitable access to health services across the social and geographical expanse of the country is the main objective of the policy. It also seeks to increase the aggregate public health investment through increased contribution from the Central as well as state governments and encourages the setting up of private insurance instruments for increasing the scope of coverage of the secondary and tertiary sector under private health insurance packages. The government envisages an increase in health expenditure as a percentage of GDP from existing 0.9% to 2.0 % by 2010 and an increase in the share of central grants from the existing 15% to constitute at least 25% of total public health spending by 2010. The State government spending for health in turn would increase from 5.5% to 7% of the budget by 2005, to be further increased to 8% by 2010. The National Population Policy (NPP) (2000), envisages the establishment of a family welfare-linked health insurance plan. As per this plan, couples living below the poverty line who undergo sterilization with not more than two living children would be eligible for insurance. Under this scheme, the couple along with their children would be covered for hospitalization not exceeding Rs 5,000 and a personal accident insurance cover for the spouse undergoing sterilization. The Institute of Health Systems (IHS), Hyderabad has been entrusted the responsibility of operationalizing the mandate of the NPP 2000. The initial scheme proposed by the HIS was discussed at a workshop in June 2003. The consensus at the meeting was that the scheme, needed further improvement prior to its implementation even as a pilot project. In keeping with the recommendations of the Tenth Five Year Plan and the National Health Policy (NHP) 2002, the Department of Family Welfare is also proposing to commission studies in eight states covering eight districts, to generate district-specific data, which is essential for conceptualization of a reasonable and financially viable insurance scheme.

The current plan – the Tenth Five Year Plan (2002-07) - also focuses on exploring alternative systems of health care financing including health insurance so that essential, need-based and affordable health care is available to all. The urgent need to evolve, implement and evaluate an appropriate scheme for health financing for different income groups is acknowledged. In the past, the government has tried to ensure that the poor get access to private health facilities through subsidy in the form of duty exemptions and other such benefits. Social health insurance for families living below the poverty line has been suggested as a mechanism for reducing the adverse economic consequences of hospitalization and treatment for chronic ailments requiring expensive and continuous care. In the budget for the year 2002-2003, an insurance scheme called *Janraskha* was introduced, with the aim of providing protection to the needy population. With a premium of Re 1/- per day, it ensured indoor treatment up to Rs 3,000 per year at selected and designated hospitals and outpatient treatment up to Rs 2,000 per year at designated clinics, including civil hospitals, medical colleges, private trust hospitals and other NGO-run *Social Health Insurance Page 95* institutions. A few states have started implementing this scheme under pilot phase.

In the budget for the period 2003-2004, another initiative of community-based health insurance has been announced. This scheme aims to enable easy access of less advantaged citizens to good health services, and to offer health protection to them. This policy covers people between the age of three months to 65 years. Under this scheme, a premium equivalent to Re 1 per day (or Rs 365 per year) for an individual, Rs 1.50 per day for a family of five (or Rs 548 per year), and Rs 2 per day for a family of seven (or Rs 730 per year), would entitle them to get reimbursement of medical expenses up to Rs 30,000 towards hospitalization, a cover for death due to accident for Rs 25,000 and compensation due to loss of earning at the rate of Rs 50 per day up to a maximum of 15 days. The government would contribute Rs 100 per year towards the annual premium, so as to ensure the affordability of the scheme to families living below the poverty line. The implementation of this scheme rests with the four public sector insurance companies. The government also offers assistance by way of Illness Assistance Funds, which have been set up by the Ministry of Health and Family Welfare at the national level and in a few states. State Illness Assistance Funds exist in Andhra Pradesh, Bihar, Goa, Gujarat, Himachal Pradesh, Jammu and Kashmir, Karnataka, Kerala, Madhya Pradesh, Maharashtra, Mizoram, Rajasthan, Sikkim,

Tamil Nadu, Tripura, West Bengal, NCT of Delhi and UT of Pondicherry. A National Illness Assistance Fund (NIAF) was set up in 1997, with the scheme being reviewed in January 1998. Through this, three Central Government hospitals and three national-level institutes have been sanctioned Rs 10,00,000 each at a time from the NIAF to provide immediate financial assistance to the extent of Rs 25,000 per case to poor patients living below the poverty line and who are undergoing treatment in these hospitals/institutions. Thereafter the scheme has been extended to few other institutes across the country and provides Rs 25,000 – Rs 50,000 per case.

Health insurance initiatives by State Governments In the recent past, various state governments have begun health insurance initiatives. For instance, the Andhra Pradesh government is implementing the *Aarogya Raksha* Scheme since 2000, with a view to increase the utilization of permanent methods of family planning by covering the health risks of the *Regional Overview in South-East Asia Page 96* acceptors. All people living below the poverty line and those who accept permanent methods of family planning are eligible to be covered under this scheme. The Government of Andhra Pradesh pays a premium of Rs 75 per acceptor. The benefits to be availed of, include hospitalization costs up to Rs. 4000 per year for the acceptor and for his/her two children for a total period of five years from date of the family planning operation. The coverage is for common illnesses and accident insurance benefits are also offered. The hospital bill is directly reimbursed by the Insurance Company, namely the New India Assurance Company.

The Government of Goa along with the New India Assurance Company in 1988 developed a medical reimbursement mechanism. This scheme can be availed by all permanent residents of Goa with an income below Rs 50 000 per annum for hospitalization care, which is not available within the government system. The non-availability of services requires certification from the hospital Dean or Director Health Services. The overall limit is Rs 30 000 for the insured person for a period of one year. A pilot project on health insurance was launched by the Government of Karnataka and the UNDP in two blocks since October 2002. The aim of the project was to develop and test a model of community health financing suited for rural community, thereby increasing the access to medical care of the poor. The beneficiaries include the entire population of these blocks. The premium is Rs 30 per person per year, with the Government of Karnataka subsidizing the premium of those below poverty line and those belonging to Scheduled Castes/ Scheduled Tribes. This premium entitles them to hospitalization coverage in the government hospitals up to a maximum of Rs 2,500 per year, including hospitalization for common illnesses, ambulance charges, loss of wages at Rs. 50 per day as well as drug expenses at Rs 50 per day. Reimbursements are made to an insurance fund which has been set up by the NGO/PRI with the support of UNDP. The Government of Kerala is planning to launch a pilot project of health insurance for the 30% families living below the poverty line. The scheme would be associated with a government insurance company. Currently, negotiations are under way with the IRA to seek service tax exemption. The proposed premium is Rs 250 plus 5% tax. The maximum benefit per family would be Rs 20 000. The amount for the premium would be recovered from the drug budget (Rs 100), the PRI (Rs 100) and from the beneficiary (Rs 62.50) *Social Health Insurance Page 97* while the benefits available would include cover for hospitalization, deliveries involving surgical procedures (either to the mother or the newborn). Instead of payment by the beneficiary, Smart Card facility would be offered. This scheme would be applicable in 216 government hospitals.

Health insurance operational costs

There is usually a substantial difference in the cost of running a private health insurance compared to a public scheme. The difference can be five to ten times lower in the case of public systems. The main reason for such differences is that public systems are compulsory. People cannot opt out of them. The cost of acquisition is thus lower. There is also a range of non-government organizations (NGOs) and self-help groups that operate their own health insurance schemes. Probably the most well known is the Indian Self-Employed Women's Association (SEWA). For members, the scheme charges an annual premium of Rupees 30 to a maximum of Rupees 1,200 per year. There is also a fixed deposit option, i.e. a set amount is deposited with a hospital irrespective of any scheme. The actual health care scheme is run (on a group basis) by the government-owned insurer – New India Assurance, and there are a number of health insurance type plans along SEWA lines.[23]

Current policies available in the market and the major players

The first policy that comes to mind is General Insurance Corporation's (GIC) Mediclaim health insurance scheme. Currently there are only two players in this field, Life Insurance Corporation and General Insurance Corporation (with its four subsidiaries). Mediclaim is the health insurance scheme offered by GIC, while Jeevan Asha is offered by Life Insurance Corporation (LIC). Competition has, however, brought in many new players. Emerging markets, comprising 86 per cent of world population, including some of the populated nations like China (1.3 billion), India (1.1 billion) and Indonesia (0.2 billion) account for 23 per cent of global economic output. Emerging markets collectively accounted for 11 per cent of global life insurance premiums in 2003.[24]

Over the next 50 years, Brazil, Russia, India and China (BRIC) could become a much larger force in the world economy. Several companies entered the health insurance market and a dozen companies linked with foreign partners. Growth in the twenty-first century will come from countries like South Korea, China, Taiwan, South Africa and India. Delay may doom the future efforts of insurance companies to stake a claim in these high potential markets.[25]

New insurance schemes

One scheme, the Universal Health Insurance policy, is available to groups of 100 or more family members. The policy reimburses up to Rs. 30000 medical expenses towards hospitalisation for the family. In cases of the family head's accidental death, Rs. 25000 compensation is paid for the loss of earnings at Rs. 50 per day, up to a maximum of 15 days, after a three-day waiting period. The premium is Rs. 365 per annum for an individual, Rs. 1.50 per day for a family of five limited to spouse and children and Rs. 2 per day for covering dependent parents in a family size up to seven. A subsidy of Rs. 100 per year towards annual premium for families below the poverty line is also provided under the scheme.

For the purposes of this policy "hospital" means:

- Any hospital/nursing home registered with the local authority and under the supervision of a registered and qualified medical practitioner.

- Hospital/nursing home run by the government.

- Enlisted hospitals run by NGOs/trusts and selected private hospitals with fixed schedule of charges.

Hospitalisation should be for a minimum period of 24 hours. However, this time limit is not applied to some specific treatments and also where, owing to technological advancement, hospitalisation for 24 hours may not be required.

The main policy exclusions are:

- All pre-existing diseases.

- Corrective, cosmetic or aesthetic dental surgery or treatment.

- Spectacles, contact lens and hearing aid.

- Primarily diagnostic expenses not related to sickness/injury.

- Treatment for pregnancy, childbirth, miscarriage, abortions etc.

- Covers people between the ages of three months to 65 years.

Under the policy, family members can receive reimbursement of Rs. 30,000 (US$656) individually or collectively.

Private insurance as a catalyst for progress

In constituting the origins of health insurance, private health schemes traditionally initiate and facilitate health care progress. Continuously seeking possibilities to improve the service offered to their clients, private health insurers are, almost by nature, social entrepreneurs. This social entrepreneurship forms the basis of the innovative added value that private health insurance may offer. In the context of increased globalisation, international challenges emerge for health insurance and health provision. Because of improved communication and travel, more people are able to purchase products and services throughout the world. Health care and health insurance cannot escape this irreversible development. This causes public health systems – national phenomena closely bound to the state, many difficulties, but insured respondents offering private health insurance have a great deal of experience and skill dealing with international cases. Flexibility enables private health insurance to offer quick solutions for emerging issues. This flexibility is one of the preconditions for private health insurance to function as a catalyst for innovation in health insurance and health care provision. In response to the waiting list problem, for example, private insurance showed a sense of innovation by offering patients rapid treatment in high quality hospitals abroad. While public health systems are mainly concerned with reimbursing or offering health care, private health insurance sector risk prevention efforts are significant. Private insurance may contribute to the development in medical science by making new technologies and medicine that are not (yet) covered by public health systems financially accessible. Finally, private health insurance is a forerunner regarding patient service informatics. In countries where medical costs are being reimbursed, the introduction of electronic medical insurance cards can lower the administrative burden for patients and providers. These and similar initiatives may be adopted by public health systems or may be left to private health insurance. Private insured respondents however have taken the first step more readily.[26]

Source: Private Health Insurance in India, Promise and Reality, 2008.

The figure above illustrates very generally the flow of information among the consumers, intermediaries, ancillary service and providers identified in the Indian health sector at present. This figure is evident by itself and shows interconnections among different sectors involved in health industry. It is important to notice that information plays a significant part in making the industry grow and help establish a trustworthy connection among the consumer and service providers.

Table 5.12: Framework for Evaluating Health Insurance in India

Characteristic	Measures/Indicators	Benchmark
Score of population covered and growth trend	Thousands of persons, individuals or families covered annual increase in percentage covered	1. Target population clearly defined 2. Growth exceeding 20% until close to saturation 3. For large groups, exceeding 50% by year 5
Scope of population covered and growth trend	Thousands of persons, individuals or families covered annual increase in percentage covered	1. Target population clearly defined 2. Growth exceeding 20% until close to saturation 3. For large groups, exceeding 50% by year 5
Covered services	Limits on coverage, including rupee amount waiting periods, pre-existing conditions, renewability, etc. Included benefits, e.g. catastrophic care, primary care and prevention	Essential basics services including primary care and prevention, hospitalization, disease management, etc.
Geographic access to care Financial access to care	Kilometers or hours of travel Lost wages/salary Costs of travel to hospital covered	Within 20 km from a PHC, within 50 km from hospital Benefits include wage loss and travel costs
Affordability – including subsidies	Annual policy cost less subsidy Average Income for Group; size of subsidy	1% to 3% of income depending on coverage
Efficiency of operations	Administrative costs, time lapsed for reimbursement or cashless, appropriate use of technology and services	Administrative costs <20% (includes all administrative ancillaries)
Cost containment	Demand side, e.g. co-pays, co-insurance, subsidies Supply sided – utilization management/physician incentives	Strong case/disease management programs; effective preauthorization and utilization review, strong provider contracts regarding quality/ cost expectations and incentives
Consumer Satisfaction Consumer Awareness and Understanding	Ability to choose among sources of care or network; other access limitations, process for resolving grievances. Actions taken by the industry, the regulator and other stakeholders to educate the public about both the advantages and the potential for misrepresentation of health insurance benefits.	Measures of consumer satisfaction tracked and actions taken to resolve complaints and improve services. Coverage clearly explained by well-trained and effective marketing personnel. Literature and other communication devices in local vernacular used to raise awareness, as applicable.

Characteristic	Measures/Indicators	Benchmark
Innovation	Market research, new products, percentage of policy-holder renewals	Consumer feedback, lessons learnt, challenges, etc. translated into innovations that improve effectiveness.
Management Attributes	Years of experience of management, HR practices Financial accounting systems in place which provide complete picture of financial situation; loss ratios and trend in loss ratios	HR plans and continuing skill improvement programs in place for all staff. Strong internal and external financial controls and accountability.
Organizational Structure Regulatory compliance	Organization chart available to beneficiaries, qualifications and determination of membership on Board of Directors, consecutive years in business. Regulations adopted for registration/licensure and performance monitoring Percent of coverage of individuals in compliant plans Sanctions in place for non-compliance with regulation	High functioning Board of Directors provides transparent and sustainable financial and beneficiary results. IRDA requires registration of all carriers of health risks and risk-pooling arrangements and all TPA activities. GOI passes enabling legislation enabling entities and/or organizations other than insurance companies to provide health insurance arrangements/schemes to individuals or groups and bring their operations under regulatory oversight. Effective enforcement in place.
Sustainability	Level of reserves Fraction of income from donors Net income/deficit Trend in net income/deficit	Long term sustainability requires buildup of resources and reserves, positive net income after year 3, and independence from donor subsidies.

The framework we use to evaluate health coverage mechanisms that rely on financial intermediaries is based upon basic policy concerns facing all health systems. A summary of these desired characteristics, suggested means of measuring the characteristics, and benchmarks against which the study team measured the current situation in India are shown in the following table.

Table 5.13: Sources of Funding for Health

Financing Agent	Expenditure in Rs. millions	% distribution
Ministry of Health and Family Welfare	24,629	2.3
Other Central Ministries/Departments	2,132	0.2
State Government Department of Health	141,699	13.4
Other State Ministries/Departments	2,311	0.2
Urban Local Bodies and Panchayat Raj Institutions	31,784	3.0
Social Security Funds	790	0.1
Central Government Employee Schemes	25,797	2.4
State Government Employee Schemes	5,119	0.5
Employee State Insurance Scheme	17,954	1.7
Public Health Insurance Providers (GIC Companies)	7,823	0.7
Private Health Insurance Providers	202	0.0
Households	744,225	70.4*
NGOs	8,540	0.8
Private Firms and Public Firms	44,336	4.3
Total funds provided	1,957,341	100.0

Source: National Health Accounts 2001-2002; No updated information on NHA
was available from the MoHFW
* Out of pocket

As presented in table, household out-of-pocket expenditure is by a wide margin the most important source of financing for health care services. However, the average amounts spent and the distribution of these expenditures across states and by urban and rural populations vary considerably. This variation, demonstrated in the tables that follow, has implications for both policies on the distribution of public states are spending and the importance of micro-insurance and other forms of health coverage as a complement to public spending.

Table 5.14: Average Monthly Per Capita Consumer Expenditure (MPCE) for Selected States and by Rural/Urban for January 2004 – June 2005

Selected States	Average MPCE in Rs. Jan-June 2004	Urban as Percentage of Rural Expenditure	Average MPCE in Rs. July 2004 – June 2005	Urban as Percentage of Rural Expenditure
Andhra Pradesh		198		174
Rural	557		586	
Urban	1102		1019	
Assam		192		195
Rural	532		543	
Urban	1019		1058	
Bihar		177		167
Rural	442		417	
Urban	784		696	
Gujarat		178		187
Rural	613		596	
Urban	1092		1115	
Karnataka		187		203
Rural	502		508	
Urban	937		1033	
Maharashtra		221		202
Rural	569		568	
Urban	1259		1148	
Orissa		211		190
Rural	414		399	
Urban	872		757	
Tamil Nadu		188		179
Rural	603		602	
Urban	1131		1080	
Uttar Pradesh		154		151
Rural	538		647	
Urban	827		978	
All India		188		188
Rural	565		559	
Urban	1060		1052	

Table 5.15: Proportion (per 1000) of persons hospitalized in rural and urban areas and population per bed in selected states

State	Rural	Urban	Population per bed
Andhra Pradesh	22	28	1057
Assam	11	16	1782
Bihar	10	10	3029
Gujarat	29	36	709
Karnataka	23	26	1319
Maharashtra	30	36	920
Orissa	23	30	3064
Tamil Nadu	37	37	1135
Uttar Pradesh	13	20	2647

As shown above in figure, the government is the single most important source of reimbursement for hospital expenses. The social insurance programs, to which government is a major contributor either through sponsorship of the scheme or public provision of covered services, are described in this section. Although they constitute only a small fraction of total health financing (estimated at about 3 percent in 2001), they are the most important sources of health insurance for families in India.[27]

Table 5.16: Number of Insured Persons and Beneficiaries under ESIS

Coverage (as per 31st March 2006)

Number of insured person family units	91,48,605
Number of employees	84,00,526
Total number of beneficiaries	3,54,96,589
Number of insured women	15,43,250
Number of employers, etc.	3,00,718

Source: NSS 60th Round. (2006). *Morbidity, Health Care and Condition of the Aged.* Report No. 507, 25.

The Central Government Health Scheme (CGHS) is a mandatory social health insurance scheme for employees and retirees of the central government. Coverage includes: OPD, emergency, drugs, lab tests, family welfare services, specialist visits, and a 90% advance for specialized procedures. In 2004, CGHS covered approximately 44 lakh people, or 0.5% of the population and according to the Ministry of Health and Family Welfare annual report, 11.44% of the total health budget (MOHFW) was spent on CGHS in 2004-2005. The total cost of CGHS has fluctuated in past six years, as has percentage of health expenditure on CGHS. At its peak in 2003-2004, CGHS was 18% of total health budget. This is in part due to CGHS allowing beneficiaries to purchase drugs at pharmacy shops and introducing contracting with private hospitals for providing healthcare to CGHS beneficiaries. However, in recent years, the expenditure on CGHS has come down dramatically (in 2005-2006 it is expected that CGHS will be 6% of the total health budget).[28]

Table 5.17: Total expenditure on CGHS (Rs. in crore) for period 1999-2006

Expenditure type	1999-2000	2001-2002	2003-2004	2004-2005	2005-2006 (outlay)
Establishment	117.1125	125.3384	139.4496	NA	NA
Supplies and materials	106.1760	1656.3858	222.9404	NA	NA
Professional services	47.8071	65.7699	140.7256	NA	NA
Total CGHS	271.0956	356.4941	503.1156	331.63	230.00
Total MOHFW budget	2132.46	2577.04	2800.64	2897.64	3801.79
% share of CGHS	12.7	13.8	18.0	11.4	6.0

Source: Rao, S. (2005). *MoHFW Annual Report 2005-2006.*

In 2004, the Central Government introduced the Universal Health Insurance (UHI) scheme, which was aimed at those living below the poverty level. The "Government Rupee-a-Day" scheme (because the annual premium is Rs 365 per person, i.e., a rupee a day), is centrally financed and implemented through the LIC and the four public sector insurance companies. The Central Government subsidizes the premium costs for the BPL[29] community by reimbursing the insurance companies after a policy has been sold to a BPL. There has been little uptake of the UHI, as can be seen from the low levels of subsidy reimbursement to the implementing insurance companies.

Table 5.18: Per 1000 distribution of persons hospitalized by type of ailment, all India

Type of ailment	Rural	Urban
Diarrhea/dysentery	76	62
Gastritis/gastric or peptic ulcer	48	39
Hepatitis/Jaundice	15	22
Heart disease	43	80
Hypertension	18	32
Respiratory including ear/nose throat ailments	35	30
Tuberculosis	30	17
Bronchial asthma	34	30
Disorders of joints and bones	25	26
Diseases of kidney/urinary system	37	49
Gynecological disorders	52	50
Neurological disorders	32	32
Psychiatric disorders	10	6
Cataract	29	24
Diabetes mellitus	18	24
Malaria	32	36
Fever of unknown origin	79	67
Locomotor disability	13	9
Accidents/injuries/burns/etc.	101	88
Cancer and other tumors	28	32
Other diagnosed ailments	164	166
Other undiagnosed ailments	19	15
Any ailment	1000	1000

*Ailments with at least 1% share are only listed separately
Source: NSS 60th Round. (2006). *Morbidity, Health Care and Condition of the Aged.* Report No. 507, 26.

Table data from 2004-05 on hospitalizations by diagnosis distinguishing between rural and urban populations also indicate a burden of disease associated with both poverty (dysentery and unknown fevers) and with more modern causes (heart disease and accidents, particularly in crowded urban areas). However, all could be mitigated through preventative strategies.

Table 5.19: Health expenditure by state government by functions

2001-2002

Health care functions	% distribution
Services of curative care	47.6
Rehabilitative or long term nursing care	0.2
Ancillary services and therapeutic appliances	1.9
Reproductive and child health services	12.2
Drugs control	0.3
Nutritional program of state department of health	0.1
Control of communicable diseases	6.2
Control of non-communicable diseases	0.4
Public health or RCH education/training	0.5
Other public health related activities	1.3
Health administration	8.4
Capital expenditure	4.7
Medical expenditure and training of health personnel	8.7
Research and development	0.2
Food adulteration	0.2
Function from other sources	7.1
Total	100

Source: NHA 2001-2002, op.cit.

As per table, according to the NHA published in 2005 (for the 2001-2002 fiscal year), 47% of the State Government health expenditure in 2001-2002 was for curative care, by far the largest segment of the State health budget.

Table 5.20: Breakdown of health premium between Government-owned and private non-life insured respondents

Name of non-life insurance company	2001-02 (Rs. Mn)	Market share	2002-03 (Rs. Mn)	Market share	2003-04 (Rs. Mn)	Market share	2004-05 (Rs. Mn)	Market share	2005-06 (Rs. Mn)	Market share
New India	2,759	36	3,544	34	3,662	30	4,797	29	6,693	30
National	1,761	23	2,253	22	2,980	24	3,186	19	3,304	15
United India	1,526	20	2,111	20	2,342	19	2,939	18	3,593	16
Oriental	1,507	19	2,041	20	2,295	19	2,735	16	3,599	16
Total Government	7,553	98	9,949	95	11,279	92	13,657	82	17,189	76
Total AIG	-	-	-	-	-	-	264	2	306	1
Royal Sundaram	42	1	96	1	161	1	297	2	499	2
ICICI Lombard	-	-	134	1	333	3	1,188	7	2,745	12
Iffco Tokio	19	0	77	1	134	1	283	2	520	2
Bajaj Allianz	123	2	120	1	227	2	706	4	976	4
Reliance	3	0	51	0	74	1	80	0	86	0
Cholamandalam	-	-	11	0	91	1	201	1	211	1
HDFC Chubb	-	-	-	-	-	-	20	0	46	0
Total Private	187	2	489	5	1,019	8	3,038	18	5,388	24
Grand Total	7,740	100	10,438	100	12,298	100	16,695	100	22,576	100

Source: IRDA with analysis

Table provides a breakdown of health premium between government-owned and private non-life insured respondents. The health insurance market share of government owned insured respondents declined from 98 per cent in 2001-02 to 76 percent in 2005-06. Conversely, the health insurance market share of private non-life insured respondents increased twelve fold from two per cent to 24 per cent during the same period.

Table 5.21: Individual and Group Insurance coverage by Government and private companies 2002-03 and 2003-04

	2002-03				2003-04			
	Lives covered (in Mn)	% of total	Premium (Rs Mn)	% of total	Lives covered (in Mn)	% of total	Premium (Rs. Mn)	% of total
Government Companies								
Individual	5.0	53	6,769	65	5.9	57	7,353	60
Group	3.6	38	3,180	30	3.8	37	3,927	32
Total	8.6	91	9,949	95	9.7	94	11,280	92
Private Companies								
Individual	0.7	7	89	1	0.1	1	205	2
Group	0.2	2	349	3	0.5	5	739	6
Total	0.9	9	489	4	0.6	6	1019	8
Combined Totals								
Individual	5.7	60	6,858	66	6.1	59	7,558	61
Group	3.8	40	3,529	34	4.3	41	4,666	38
Grand Total	9.5	100	10,438	100	10.3	100	12,298	100

Source: IRDA with analysis

Table 5.22: Bajaj Allianz's Silver Health Premium Rates

(Figures in Rs.)

Sum Insured	Annual Premium					
	Age (in years)					
	46-50	51-55	56-60	61-65	66-70	71-75
50,000	1,995	2,495	3,824	4,780	7,170	8,963
100,000	2,993	3,742	5,736	7,170	10,755	13,444
150,000	3,741	4,677	7,170	8,963	13,444	16,805
200,000	4,676	5,846	8,963	11,203	16,805	21,006
300,000	5,845	7,308				

Source: IRDA with analysis

Table for Premium details: Bajaj Allianz recently introduced its Silver Health policy, primarily aimed at senior citizens. It is a unique but high cost product since it covers individuals between the ages of 46 and 75 years. With insured respondents putting restrictions on entry age for their health plans, this is the only plan specifically designed for older persons.

Table 5.23: Health insurance premium rate comparisons of non-life insured respondents

Age/Insurance Company (years)	Star Health	Bajaj Allianz	IFFCO Tokio	Govt. owned	Reliance	Royal Sundaram	Oriental
20	1,200	1,254	1,098	1,310	1,310	985	1,179
30	1,200	1,453	1,195	1,310	1,310	1,692	1,310
40	1,350	1,453	1,441	1,425	1,425	1,692	1,566
50	2,447	2,793	2,116	2,039	2,039	2,275	2,447
60	3,000	-	2,783	2,322	2,322	3,277	3,483
70	4,547	-	3,396	2,598	2,598	4,719	5,196
80	6,029	-	-	3,445	3,445	-	6,960

Premiums indicated are in Rs and are for a benefit limit of Rs. 100,000
Source: Indian Express. "60-plus, don't come to us!" September, 2006.

According to table, there are also significant differences in the individual purchase market, comparing health insurance premium rates for the hospitalization products among non-life insurers by age. The premium rate per annum for a benefit limit of Rs 100,000 ranges from approximately one per cent of the insured amount for 20-year-olds to seven per cent of the insured amount for an 80-year-old person.[30]

Table 5.24: Percentage of insured making claims per year

Benefit limit/year	1st year	2nd year	3rd year	4th year onward
Upto Rs. 50,000	33%	20%	15%	32%
Rs.50,000 to Rs.100,000	20%	15%	12%	53%
Rs. 100,000 & above	13%	10%	10%	67%

Source: A government-owned non-life insurance company.

Table 5.25: Comparison of premium rates (CHNBHA vs. Oriental Insurance Company's Mediclaim Policy)

(Figures in Rs.)

Sum insured	Mediclaim Premium Rates Age					CHNHBA Premium above 18 years
	20 years	46 yeas	56 years	61 years	>70 years	
50,000	609	1,265	1,799	2,688	3,600	1,000
100,000	1,179	2,447	3,483	5,196	6,960	1,565
200,000	2,221	4,680	6,687	10,018	13,678	3,850
250,000	2,660	5,672	8,133	12,222	16,778	4,400
300,000	3,100	6,664	9,581	14,428	19,878	4,950
400,000	3,867	8,483	12,267	18,562	25,735	6,600

Source: A government-owned non-life insurance company.

Table 5.26: CHNHBA Health insurance policy – Premium and coverage

(Figures in Rs.)

Schedule	Annual premium per member		Total coverage	
	Age upto 18 years	Age over 18 years		
I	350	430	30,000	With sub-limits
II	720	900	60,000	With sub-limits
III	1,200	1,440	1,15,000	With sub-limits
IV	1,020	1,200	60,000	Without sub-limits
V	1,560	1,800	1,15,000	Without sub-limits
VI	3,630	3,850	2,00,000	Without sub-limits
VII	4,180	4,400	2,50,000	Without sub-limits
VIII	4,730	4,950	3,00,000	Without sub-limits
IX	6,380	6,600	4,00,000	Without sub-limits

Source: Revised premium rates in effect from 2006.

Table 5.27: Overview of the current Ashwini Health Insurance Scheme

Characteristic	Description
Owner and manager of the scheme	ACCORD, a non-governmental organization, set up by the Association for Health Welfare in the Nilgiris (ASHWINI)
Administration of health insurance scheme	ACCORD manages premiums; ASHWINI manages claims
Distribution and marketing	ACCORD, ASHWINI and the Adivasi Munnetra Sangam (AMS) field staff all collect enroll, renew, and collect premiums
Service providers	Three-tier delivery system which begins at the village level with trained tribal health workers. ASHWINI has a network of seven regional health sub-centers manned by adivasi nursing assistants and the Gudalur Adivasi Hospital which also serves as the main ASHWINI administrative center. Referrals are made to tertiary centers at Kozhikode or Coimbatore as needed.
Role of state government	Government of Tamil Nadu provides some assistance for certain programs: immunization (free vaccinations), family planning (incentives for sterilization), TB program (testing kits and medicines), and sickle cell program (supplies for testing)
Starting date	1992
Insurance term	Annual term beginning April 15th of every year
Participation	Voluntary enrolment of individuals and families
Insured unit	Annual coverage on an individual basis
Risk pooling	ASHWINI/ACCORD informally assumes part of the risk; partnered with Royal Sundaram Alliance (RSA); originally with New India Assurance Corporation (NIAC) 1992-2002 (see below)
Target marketing	Adivasis (tribal people) residing in Gudalur taluk in Nilgiri District, Tamil Nadu
Eligibility requirements	Ages 0-60; must be member of AMS
Annual premium rates	Rs. 40 per person per year (2006)
Benefits	Royal Sundaram Alliance Insurance Company (RSA): • Coverage of Rs. 2500 per person per year • All deliveries and pregnancy related admissions are allowed • For delivery related admissions a ceiling of Rs. 1000 per case ASHWINI insurance program: • All hospitalization costs above Rs. 2500, with no limits • Outpatient care • Drug costs • Public health/Preventative services • Maternity beyond RSA benefit
Exclusions	RSA: • Psychiatric conditions • Self-inflicted injuries
Claims settlement	15-20 days under RSA; it was 3-9 months under NIAC
Waiting period	None
Co-payment	Everyone pays a Rs. 10 administration fee upon hospitalization; AMS members who have not paid the premium to ACCORD pay Rs. 100 per hospitalization; non-AMS members pay Rs. 150 per hospitalization plus other fees.
Availing benefits	Cashless system, but varies as follows: • AMS members who have not paid premium can access services at ASHWINI hospital and sub-centers by paying user fees/co-payments. • AMS member who have paid annual premium are enrolled in ASHWINI insurance scheme and receive free care at the health facilities. • Non-AMS members can also use services in the ASHWINI health facilities, but pay higher user fees.
Financing	Participants' premiums Reimbursements from RSA User fees charged at the hospital Donor and philanthropist financing

Source: Devadasan, N., et al. (2004).

As per table, quite encouraged by the success of the community health programme and the role played by the adivasi health workers, the adivasi community felt that the next logical step would be to start a hospital of our own. There was a heavy demand from the village sangams to start a hospital. But the doctors were reluctant, saying that Hospital is a permanent institution which needs to be run 24 hours a day, all through the year - and for many years. The health team at that time was not equipped to handle such an institution. Moreover, the ACCORD team strongly felt that their intervention had to be time-bound and they will withdraw after a few years when the AMS can take over the initiative of protecting the rights of the adivasis.[31]

Table 5.28: Features of the current BASIX health insurance program

Characteristic	Description
Owner and manager of the scheme	BASIX, a for-profit, non-governmental organization
Administrator and TPA	BASIX manages claims processing but out-sources to a company (BPO) to verify documents submitted to support claims
Distribution and marketing	Consumers are educated at the point of borrowing; field staff also go to households which have experienced an insured events to discuss the claims process in the vicinity of family and other potential clients
Service providers	Beneficiaries can use health services at any public or private facility
Role of the state government	NA
Starting date	2005 (for health; 2002 for life insurance products)
Insurance term	Duration of the loan repayment; if client is delinquent on repayment of loan for 180 days, insurance is cancelled
Scope of operation	Eleven states
Participation	All those who use BASIX credit services are allowed to participate for a nominal monthly premium rate and receive benefits immediately
Insured unit	Coverage for borrower and spouse
Risk pooling	Risk is borne by the insurance company, Royal Sundaram Alliance
Target market	Productive BPL borrowers of BASIX
Eligibility requirements	Qualification for getting a loan from BASIX, limited to age 18-54
Annual premium rates	Rs. 68 per person per month (136 per couple)
Premium collection	Monthly when loan repayment is made at specified community locations Grameena Arogya Raksha Critical illness: Rs. 10,000 Permanent total disability: Rs. 25,000 Hospital cash: Rs. 300 per day upto Rs. 1,500 (5 days per annum) SHG Parivaar Beena Life: Rs. 20,000 PTD: Rs. 20,000 Hospital cash: Rs. 1,500
Exclusions	None
Claims settlement Waiting period Co-payment and user fees Availing benefits	Done at BASIX; approximately 50-60 days for reimbursement to the insured. No waiting period None No pre-authorization necessary; beneficiaries can use services at any health facility (public or private) and apply for reimbursement
Financing	Premiums to the insurance company; beneficiaries are also charged Rs. 10 per person, which covers the cost of administration of the schemes

Source: BASIX 10th Annual Report, 2006.

Table 5.29: Overview of the Grameen Arogya Raksha component of BASIX

Target clients	Rural credit customers of BASIX and their spouses
Insurer	Royal Sundaram
Group or individual?	Group
Policy holder	BSFL
Minimum entry age	18 years last birthday
Maximum age	54 years last birthday; exit age is 55
Policy benefits and sum insured	Critical illness: Rs. 10,000 PTD: Rs. 25,000 Hospital cash: Rs. 300 per day upto Rs. 1,500 (5 days per annum)
Exclusion and waiting period	30 days waiting period for claiming hospital cash
Premium rate	Rs. 68 per year per person. Premium is paid monthly
Frequency of premium payment to insurance company	Monthly, with loan installment
Coverage period	From disbursement date to last date of the month in which loan is closed. Coverage stops when loan repayment is overdue by 180 days from the last payment schedule date
Medical check-up	Not required

Source: BASIX 10th Annual Report, 2006.

In March 2006, BASIX began offering a health insurance benefit for the Self Health Group Parivaar Beema, which is a combination product and covers risks for: life, total and permanent disability due to accident, and hospital cash to cover expenses for hospitalization. It is offered through the Indian Grameen Services, which is one of the subsidiary companies offering credit and savings options for SHGs. Royal Sundaram Alliance is providing the coverage for the health portion of the product while AVIVA covers the life portion. The premium for this product is Rs 372 per year per member and it covers both the member and the spouse. Details are summarized above.

CGHS has health facilities in 24 cities having 246 Allopathy Dispensaries and Total 438 Dispensaries in the Country with 847081 registered cards/families.

Number of C.G.H.S. Dispensaries (Alopathic) in different cities

Source: BASIX 10th Annual Report, 2006.

During 2009-10 the city wise number of CGHS beneficiaries has been analysed and presented in the graph.

Number of C.G.H.S. beneficiaries in different cities

(as on 31.3.2010)

CHAPTER – VI

FINDINGS, SUGGESTIONS AND CONCLUSIONS

6.1 MAJOR FINDINGS OF THE STUDY

Demography

- Most of the respondents were from the age group of 41-50 years, followed by 51-60 years and least were found in the age group of 20-30 years.

- Majority of the sample selected were male respondents and remaining were female respondents.

- Most of the respondents were found to have education level graduation and above.

- The family size of the respondents was dominated by 4-6 members per family, followed by 1-3 members and least were found in above 7 members group.

Health economics

- Insured respondents had higher levels of annual income, compared to non-insured respondents.

- The annual health expenditure of the insured candidates was higher than non-insured respondents.

- Majority of the insured respondents invested less than Rs. 1 lakh for health insurance.

Issues related to health insurance

- Most of the insured respondents got the awareness from employers and representatives, whereas most of the non-insured respondents got awareness through their friends.

162

- Majority of the Insured respondents met their expenditure by earning followed by other sources.

- Most of the insured respondents were found be either government employees or agriculturists, whereas most of the non insured respondents were found to be either laborers or agriculturists.

- Almost 2/3 of the selected non inured respondents were aware of medical insurance.

- Majority of the non-insured respondents felt that Government hospital treatment is sufficient to meet their health service and on the whole 54.1% of them were aware of Yashaswini scheme.

- Majority of the insured respondents opined that Health insurance gives a great relief to them and their family.

Health care services

- On the whole, 47.0% of the insured respondents had private insurance, followed by 31.5% of them possessed government insurance, 21% of them had mixed plan and very few of them had union group insurance. .

- The respondents felt that hospital unit has more difficulty for health care services had been most difficult service to available, followed by pharmacy, radiology, laboratory, other centers and least of clinic problems.

- A large majority of the respondents possessed all types of insurance to cover their needs.

- The insured premium amount was more in the categories of <1 lakh and 1-2 lakhs and payment and premiums paid were mostly annual.

- Majority of the insured sample had cashless card for health expenditure.

Utility of health insurance

- A large majority of the sample indicated that Health insurance provides or pays Hospital outpatient and hospital stay.

- Majority of the insured respondents indicated that Health insurance provide or pay Hospital Doctor visits, long term care/nursing home and dental care.

- As far as the payment on prescribed drugs are concerned, majority indicated negatively towards health insurance.

Attitude towards health insurance

- On the whole we find that insured respondents had favorable attitude towards health insurance than non-insured respondents.

- In individual areas like availability, time spent, expenditure and treatment issues also those with health insurance were more favorable compared to non- insured respondents.

Problems

- More than 50% of the respondents indicated that they had most difficult in health insurance policy Reclaiming and 48% of them indicated difficulty sometime in policy documentation.

- Majority of the sample indicated difficulty sometime for policy delay and access to health care services sometime by 43% of the respondents.

- 41.5% of the respondents indicated high premium sometime as difficulty, and 43% them indicated difficult in health insurance policy Prolonged hospitalization sometime.

- 43% and 44.5% of them indicated sometime difficulty in in health insurance policy Prolonged hospitalization and health insurance policy prolonged discharge procedure respectively.

6.2 VERIFICATION OF THE HYPOTHESES

H1: Insured respondents vary significantly in their opinion on the health economics regarding health insurance for the following
   a. Income
   b. Expenditure
   c. Amount invested on health insurance

H1 stated as "Insured respondents vary significantly in their opinion on the health economics regarding health insurance" for income is accepted as we find that insured respondents and non-insured respondents differed significantly in their annual income. It was evident that insured respondents had significantly higher income levels compared to non-insured ones.

Further, it was observed that even expenditure of health care and health issues, again it was found that insured respondents spent more money on health insurance and health issues compared to non insured ones.

Even in investing on health insurance was analyzed, it was found that insured respondents varied significantly in their investment on health insurance, where we find that majority of them were insured for less than 1 lakh rupees.

Low income is a major contributor to higher incidence and severity of illness and earlier deaths. Many low-income people have difficulty paying for health care doctor and medications when they struggle to pay for other essentials, such as housing, food and utilities. Families with lower incomes tend to live in substandard housing, have less access to healthy food options, and have greater risk factors for chronic disease than those with higher income levels.

H2: Demographic variables of insured respondents have significant influence over health insurance issues

H2 stated as 'Demographic variables of insured respondents have significant influence over health insurance issues' is partially accepted as the test statistics revealed significant influence of demographic variable on some health insurance issues as well as non-significant influence of demographic variable on some health insurance issues.

Education as a demographic variable had a significant influence over health insurance related issues where we find that on the whole those who were insured possessed higher qualification compared to non-insured respondents. Further, family size of the respondents was also found to have significant influence over health insurance related issues where we find that non-insured respondents had significantly more lower sized families compared to insured respondents.

As far the meeting expenditure is considered, it was found that insured ones met the expenditure more from earnings where as non-insured respondents met the expenditure from other sources. Occupation wise influence was found to significant, where non-insured respondents were mostly from labour class and private employees where as among insured respondents we find more of respondents from government sector.

When awareness was verified across the respondents, though majority of them had awareness about health insurance, it was observed that non-insured respondents had lesser levels of awareness compared to insured respondents. Further, expenditure analysis revealed that insured respondents spent more money on their health annually compared to non-insured respondents. Further, knowledge regarding health insurance indicated that insured respondents got more information from employers, where as non insured respondents indicated friends as the major source of information for awareness of medical insurance.

However, demographic variables like age and gender did not have significant influence over health insurance related issues.

Changes in age composition of the population will affect needs and demand for health and social care. Care needs are not evenly divided among age groups in the population. Cost per capita tends to rise sharply with age.

H3: Insured respondents vary in their opinion on claiming health insurance and other aspects

H3 stated as 'Insured respondents vary in their opinion on claiming health insurance and other aspects' is partially accepted as we find that insured respondents vary significantly in their opinion on claiming health insurance and other aspects. It was found that Only 35.0% of the sample indicated that they have Claimed any amount from the insurance company, 80.0% of them indicated Insurance Claimed Hurdle-free, 36.0% of them opined Health Insurance coverage pre existing and existing diseases, 96.5% of them indicated Health Insurance is necessary to get treatment, only 27.0% of them were member of the Yashaswini scheme, 84.5% of the respondents want to introduce Yashaswini to others, 35.5% of them indicated Problem in getting the reimbursement from insurance companies and 96.0% of them indicated they have heard of health insurance companies.

Further analysis revealed that there were moderate level of difficulty existed in reclaiming, in documentation, health insurance policy Delay in time, health insurance policy Access to health care services, health insurance policy Ability to pay, health insurance policy Drugs shortage, health insurance policy

High premium, health insurance policy prolonged hospitalization and health insurance policy prolonged discharge procedure

H4: Insured respondents face several hurdles in claiming, documentation related issues

H4 stated as 'Insured respondents face several hurdles in claiming, documentation related issues' is partially accepted. It was found that more than 50% of the respondents indicated that they had most difficult in health insurance policy Reclaiming and 48% of them indicated difficulty sometime in policy documentation. Majority of the sample indicated difficulty sometime for policy delay and access to health care services sometime by 43% of the respondents. 41.5% of the respondents indicated high premium sometime as difficulty, and 43% them indicated difficult in health insurance policy Prolonged hospitalization sometime. 43% and 44.5% of them indicated sometime difficulty in health insurance policy Prolonged hospitalization and health insurance policy prolonged discharge procedure respectively.

Except for the difficulty either most of the time or all the time policy reclaiming, the other problems seem to be quite lesser among insured respondents. This is a quite positive development, where we find that insured respondents faced difficulties or problems only for sometime. This may be due to the RTI act, strong legal action against service providers if they decline genuine claim etc. However, majority of the respondents felt that they had difficulty in immediate claims in health insurance.

It is an unfortunate occurrence when insurance problems prevent the natural progression of processing a claim that allows the insured respondents to get back to his/her life. When insurance agencies sign up for the policy it's absolutely imperative that one should read the entire policy in order to understand the limitations. However, there are plenty of times when even adhering to the limitation and restrictions that the insurance company doesn't do the fair and right thing. In order to maintain their bottom line, insurance adjusters are trained at how to effectively deny or stall claims. This is especially true when the loss causes serious physical damage or consequences to the victim. The adjuster will look at every possible angle to prevent the victim from collecting the full amount that is due to them. Illegal stall tactics are not uncommon. In fact, most people who have ended up finally receiving a settlement had to prove the legitimacy of their damage for one to three years before the settlement was funded. Since most of the insured respondents are not lawyers, they will make the assumption that the insured respondents do not know the difference between legal and illegal action on their part. The insurer may be given false information, denied timely payment, or in some worker's compensation cases sent to a physician paid to clear the claimant to return to work.

H5: Insured respondents and non-insured respondents differ significantly in their attitude/perception towards health insurance with special reference to
   a. Accessibility
   b. Time spent
   c. Cost of health care services

The hypothesis which was formulated as 'insured respondents will have favorable attitude towards health insurance' had been accepted as all the test statistics revealed that insured respondents had favorable attitude than non-insured respondents. Some of the studies on health issues revealed the following. Prasanta Mahapatra, et al. (2001) have identified in their work that, Corruption by all categories of staff was the greatest cause for dissatisfaction, followed by general cleanliness, poor utilities etc. Also significantly high level of dissatisfaction was noted regarding patient's assessment of technical quality of doctor's work and less time spent by the doctor with the patients, which are the main causes for people to go for private healthcare organizations, where majority of patients who come for treatment to public hospital are poor and illiterate. Ambuj Bharadwaj, et al. (2001) estimate that the private sector Hospitals have come up to provide the health care in a large way and this sector shares a major part of GDP 4.7% compared to 1.2% of public sector. 78.4% of total expenditure on health is shared by private sector, while 20% is accounted for by public sector. Purohit and Siddiqui (1994) examined the utilization of health services in India by making the comparison of Indian states in terms of low, medium and high household expenditure on health care and concluded that there is no serious government initiative to encourage utilization of health services by means of devising health insurance.

From the results section it is very much evident that most of the respondents under the insurance category were more favorable towards the availability component of health insurance compared to non-insured respondents.. In the case of spending time also, most of the respondents under the insurance category were more favorable towards the time spending component of health insurance compared to non-insured respondents. As far as the expenditure component is verified, again it was found that respondents under the insurance category were more favorable towards the expenditure component of health insurance compared to non-insured respondents. In the case of treatment issues a significant difference was observed in the perception among insured respondents and non-insured respondents, where it was revealed that respondents under the insurance category were more favorable towards the treatment issues component of health insurance compared to non-insured respondents.

The Affordable Care Act ensures health plans offered in the individual and small group markets, both inside and outside of the Health Insurance Marketplace, offer a comprehensive package of items and services, known as essential health benefits. Essential health benefits must include items and services within at least the following 10 categories: ambulatory patient services; emergency services; hospitalization; maternity and newborn care; mental health and substance use disorder services, including behavioral health treatment; prescription drugs; rehabilitative and habilitative services and devices; laboratory services; preventive and wellness services and chronic disease management; and pediatric services, including oral and vision care. Insurance policies must cover these benefits in order to be certified and offered in the Health Insurance Marketplace. States expanding their Medicaid programs must provide these benefits to people newly eligible for Medicaid.

Health insurance benefits in India have become indispensable for every individual keeping in mind the rising medical cost. Medical emergency can strike anyone, anytime leaving you devastated emotionally as well as financially. Though one cannot provide coverage for emotional loss, financial losses during a medical emergency can be certainly covered with a health insurance policy. Simply put a health insurance policy provides financial security to individuals during the most critical time when he/she requires funds for survival. India today is one of the fastest developing economies and people have enough amounts at disposal and savings. However, no rational individual will be willing to shell his/her hard earned money as medical expenses. Also depending upon the generosity of your friends and relatives during such trying times might just prove to be a costly affair. Thus it is in times like these that a Mediclaim Policy provides a financial helping hand and assures complete peace of mind for the insured and his family.

Medical treatment cost has reached an all time high and is further expected to rise. During a medical emergency, life is always given priority over money and thus no half measures are taken to avail the best possible treatment to the patient. Thus in absence of a health insurance policy, your hard earned money is drained in no time and many a times results in a financial crisis situation.

In light of the fiscal crisis facing the government at both central and state levels, in the form of shrinking public health budgets, escalating health care costs coupled with demand for health care services, and lack of easy access of people from the low-income group to quality health care, health insurance is emerging as an alternative mechanism for financing of health care. Health insurance in a narrow sense would be 'an individual or group purchasing health care coverage in advance by paying a fee called *premium*'. In its broader sense, it would be any arrangement that helps to defer, delay, reduce or altogether avoid paying for health care incurred by individuals and households. Given the appropriateness of this definition in the Indian context, this is the definition, we would adopt. The health insurance market in India is very limited covering about 10% of total population and has to be spread for more population including tribal and rural population.

6.3 GENERAL DISCUSSION

Health Insurance Benefits and Tax Benefits in India

In order to promote health insurance in India, the government has introduced impressive tax benefits on health insurance under Sec. 80D of the IT Act on the premium paid for a health insurance policy. Though tax benefits for Health Insurance are available with a health insurance policy most people in India are inclined towards buying health insurance policy with the sole motive of a risk cover.

Choosing the right health insurance

Health Insurance policy can be either purchased for an individual known as 'Individual health insurance policy' or the entire family known as 'Family Floater policy'. The health insurance policy is further classified into a 'Mediclaim policy' and 'Critical illness policy'. A Mediclaim policy provides coverage to the insured when he/she is hospitalized due to sickness, disease or accident. However, a critical illness policy provides coverage to the insured only if he/she is diagnosed with a pre-defined critical illness. An insured has an option to include critical illness rider in his/her Mediclaim policy to further enhance the risk cover.

Health insurance in one of the most booming sectors in India as more and more people are becoming aware of the advantages associated with it. This has invited many potential health insurance providers in the market, introducing health insurance policies with impressive features and benefits. Thus one should select a policy with maximum benefits and which fulfills most of the requirements.

Nowadays we are witnesses of open debates on the sustainability, equity and efficiency of health care systems. Health care systems face pressure to increase the quality of health care at the same time with pressure to reduce public spending. As a response to these problems developing, Central and Eastern European countries (CEE countries) have implemented large-scale market oriented health care reforms (Nemec & Kolisnichenko, 2006). Market-modeled restructuring of public institutions has dramatically transformed the organization and delivery of health services. Managerial ideologies and organizational mechanisms to enhance efficiency, accountability and competition have come to dominate their activities (Aronson & Smith, 2010). These changes resulted in narrowing the redistributive capacity of the state, de-politicizing the public realm and reducing citizenship entitlements. Unfortunately these reforms have not fully met the expectations. In Croatia, as in other developing countries, in recent decades, we have witnessed a dramatic offloading and reducing health services and programmes. In their place there are several dispersed state, regulated by governments from a distance, funders and accreditors through a range of accountancy and surveillance strategies. In these mixed economies of public and private welfare, the professional and administrative organizational cultures characteristic of the welfare state has been displaced by the ideology and distinctive practices of managerialism.

PUBLIC-PRIVATE PARTNERSHIP AS AN ANSWER TO CHALLENGES THAT FACE HEALTH CARE SYSTEMS

The market alone, in the case of comprehensive privatization, cannot answer most of the problems related to health care delivery. The attempt to overcome the gap between the needs and opportunities in the health care systems can be resolved through the introduction of public-private partnerships (PPP). The term public-private partnership refers to forms of cooperation between public authorities and the world of business which aim to ensure the funding, construction, renovation, management or maintenance of an infrastructure or the provision of a service (Commission of the European Communities, 2004). In order to ensure that health care systems continue to generate improved health care outcomes at a sustainable cost, changes are required in primary care, where providers have a role of gatekeepers. The necessity to adapt to a complex new environment places severe strains on primary care providers who deal with the lack of basic organizational and financial skills to run their practice as an integrated health business. At that point, private investors and health insured respondents recognize their interest in involvement in the provision of those services. Private entities see their investment as something that will be profitable in the long run. They see opportunities for value creation, for patients as well as for companies (OECD, 2011). According to that, on the level of the whole health care system, a private entity is more likely to offer more-profitable services, i.e. services for young and healthy people and lucrative services (Kordić & Arnerić, 2012). This study seeks to examine the contributions of socioeconomic and demographic environment contexts on the private providers of general/family health services in primary health care. Pristaš et al. (2009) in their paper argued that different mixtures of public and private financing and providing services have been introduced in developing countries, and despite existing universal coverage not all population groups have equal positions in case of equal health needs.

6.4 SUGGESTIONS OF THE STUDY

- There is an urgent need for Medicare reforms. Younger population should be brought under it at the earliest. Without which, the health status of the Indian population is likely to decline.

- Central and State Government run programmes should be more on the lines that provide with age, economic conditions appropriate and culturally proficient health care will likely alter patterns of health care to meet the needs of diverse population.

- The Central Government must focus more on providing increased support for public health programs designed to address health care knowledge, prevention, treatment adherence and barriers related to culture, language and health literacy will likely contribute for improving the health status of the population.

- The need for Public-Private Partnership is needed in improving access to medical care and addressing the underlying determinants are necessary to aid the growing number of people with chronic disease in making appropriate health decisions and adhere to physician treatment plans.

- Non Governmental Organisations must be encouraged to conduct health impact assessments to ascertain key information related to the effects of public policies (e.g., housing or transportation). These may be essential in promoting positive health outcomes and minimizing adverse health outcomes.

- Efforts must be made to strengthen the education system and labour market will have major implications for the nation's economy as well as negative consequences for the health status of the nation.

- Increasing investment by both the Government and private players are needed to provide support for the public health infrastructure and promoting collaboration between physician practices and community health resources may improve health outcomes as well as reduce health care spending related to preventable illness.

- Education of the health insured about insurance policy and the coverage is necessary so that when they are told that they cannot get the care they need, they have to ask for the reason in writing.

- Prompt action by the insurer is advised, as, any delay by more than 6 months, he/she may lose the right to file a complaint, they have to ask for an I M R, or take other action against your health plan.

- Awareness about the common problems encountered by the insured respondents has to be made available in the media. The websites of the insured respondents have to publish a Frequently Encountered Problems and suggest solutions for the same.

- Direct settlement with the major hospitals by the Insurance companies is suggested. Firms such as Bajaj Allianz, Cholamandalam MS and Star Health have opted for direct settlement of claims, eliminating TPAs.

- Insured respondents must visit hospitals to meet patients for claims under group insurance schemes. If found at fault, the group insurer should refuse to renew the policy of the originator company.

- Insured respondents must go for pre-agreed rates for surgeries and treatments. This prevents differential tariffs for the insured and uninsured patients. The hospital should bill extra charges directly to the patient.

- The insured must read the entire policy document before taking a policy. They have to ask their salesperson for the 'policy wordings'. One should not make a false claim as he/she may not be able to make a genuine second claim in the same year if the limit has been exhausted. Also, the insurer may load future premiums in case of an abnormal claim.

- Prospective clients should ask for more information. Insurance Regulatory Directorate Agency's intervention in making brochures and other promotional material more transparent will help.

The above are some of the solutions to avoid the delay in claims or other procedural difficulties.

6.5 CONCLUSIONS

It is very clear that health insurance as such is not covered for all the individuals in and around Mysore city. Roughly it is estimated that less than 20% of the individuals are possessing health insurance in some or the other form, be it voluntary or state sponsored. Where as in developed countries all the citizens are comprehensively covered under health insurance, which is compulsory too. The awareness of health insurance is very much limited among individuals especially in rural areas. Then again, there are several classes of persons who have not been brought into the insurance schemes of the government, nor have they sought health insurance voluntarily. The government should make policies regarding compulsory insurance for all the individuals as the expenditure in advanced health care and corporate hospitals is very high. This is beyond the affordability by individuals with medium and low socioeconomic status. Since health is very important in an individuals' life, the insurance coverage for diseases and surgical procedures should lower expenditure and as well be affordable at super speciality corporate hospitals also.

Though government has provided some form of health insurance in the form of "Yashaswini scheme" it is highly limited. The results of the present study clearly indicated that only people with high socioeconomic status could afford to health insurance and not the individuals with low socioeconomic status.

Except for the difficulty encountered at the time of claims settlement, the other problems seem to be quite minimal among responses of health insured. This is a positive development, where we find that health insured faced difficulties or problems only for some time. Particularly, only after obtaining the appropriate medical treatment. This may be attributed to the Right To Information Act, which provides with the transparency and removes the arbitrariness of the allowing of the claims. Any deviation on the part of the health insurance company would lead to strong legal action against service providers if they decline genuine claim etc. However, majority of the respondents felt that they had difficulty in immediate claims in health insurance.

It is an unfortunate occurrence when insurance problems prevent the natural progression of processing a claim that allows the insured to get back to his/her health. When insurance agencies sign up for the policy it's absolutely imperative that one should read the entire policy in order to understand the limitations. However, there are several occasions when even adhering to the limitation and restrictions that the insurance company doesn't do the fair and right thing. In order to maintain their profit quotient, insurance adjusters are trained at methods to effectively deny or stall claims. This is especially true when the loss causes serious physical damage or consequences to the victim. The adjuster will look at every possible angle to prevent the victim from collecting the full amount that is due to them. Illegal stall tactics are not uncommon. In fact, most people who have ended up finally receiving a settlement had to prove the legitimacy of their damage for one to three years before the settlement was funded. Since most of the insured are not lawyers, they will make the assumption that the insurer does not know the difference between legal and illegal action on their part. The insurer may be given false information, denied timely payment. However, it is desirable to have more insurance coverage to all the citizens, where they have a cover to be under, in case of any type of an illness and loss of health.

More work is needed to know the full extent of the problems and the solutions for them in the health insurance sector in India. This work is one step towards the direction and hope it paves the way for several more studies. It is hoped that this study will open the path to take up to several more studies and eventually, lead to awareness on good health, insurance to retain it and above all, being insured to face any health related setbacks. Health is wealth and a healthy nation need not be a wealthy nation. The participation of citizens, governments, non government agencies and the private players can assure an insured population, that does not have to face serious economic difficulties while also facing health related difficulties. Particularly country like India where people are more susceptible for chronic diseases like diabetic, cardiac, etc. are in need of health insurance to be free from health problems.

Milton Keynes UK
Ingram Content Group UK Ltd.
UKHW020927231123
433129UK00016B/919